CUMBRIA LIBRARIES

3800304671560 3

KT-523-278

WITHDRAWN

Nearer the Heart's Desire

BY THE SAME AUTHOR

Henry Thoreau: A Life of the Mind
Emerson: The Mind on Fire
William James: In the Maelstrom of American Modernism
First We Read, Then We Write: Emerson on the Creative Process
Splendor of Heart: Walter Jackson Bate and the Teaching of Literature
Edward FitzGerald's Rubaiyat of Omar Khayyam (introduction
and notes by Robert D. Richardson and art by Lincoln Perry)

Nearer the Heart's Desire

Poets of the Rubaiyat: A Dual Biography of Omar Khayyam and Edward FitzGerald

Robert D. Richardson

BLOOMSBURY

NEW YORK · LONDON · OXFORD · NEW DELHI · SYDNEY

Bloomsbury USA
An imprint of Bloomsbury Publishing Plc

1385 Broadway	50 Bedford Square
New York	London
NY 10018	WC1B 3DP
USA	UK

www.bloomsbury.com

BLOOMSBURY and the Diana logo are trademarks of Bloomsbury
Publishing Plc

First published 2016

© Robert D. Richardson 2016

All rights reserved. No part of this publication may be reproduced or
transmitted in any form or by any means, electronic or mechanical,
including photocopying, recording, or any information storage or retrieval
system, without prior permission in writing from the publishers.

No responsibility for loss caused to any individual or organization acting
on or refraining from action as a result of the material in this publication
can be accepted by Bloomsbury or the author.

ISBN   HB: 978-1-62040-653-3
        ePub: 978-1-62040-655-7

LIBRARY OF CONGRESS CATALOGING-IN-PUBLICATION DATA HAS BEEN
APPLIED FOR.

2 4 6 8 10 9 7 5 3 1

Typeset by RefineCatch Limited, Bungay, Suffolk
Printed and bound in USA by Berryville Graphics Inc.,
Berryville, Virginia

To find out more about our authors and books visit www.bloomsbury.com.
Here you will find extracts, author interviews, details of forthcoming
events and the option to sign up for our newsletters.

Bloomsbury books may be purchased for business or promotional use.
For information on bulk purchases please contact Macmillan Corporate
and Premium Sales Department at specialmarkets@macmillan.com.

For Annie one more time

CONTENTS

PART II

AUTHOR'S NOTE

There was no center to Edward FitzGerald's life, as his collected works, his letters, and half a dozen biographies make clear. John Banville has observed, in *Ancient Light*, that "all biographies are . . . mendacious." This one, insofar as it is a biography, is no exception. I have deliberately put the *Rubaiyat* at the center, arranging everything else around it, like potatoes around a roast. The question for a biography is not, "is it true?" It can't be true. The question should be, "is it useful?" I have not invented anything, I have not falsified any detail, at least not knowingly, but I have selected material with an eye to showing that a writer's life may have a great accomplishment to its credit even if the writer in question never fully saw it, or allowed himself to accept it, or organized his life for it.

I am grateful to Coleman Barks, who thought I could do it; to Lincoln Perry, who realized the visual links between the worlds of eleventh-century Persia, nineteenth-century England, and contemporary America; and to Alireza Taghdarreh, whose translation of *Walden* into Persian demonstrates how the Silk Road of the mind is now a two-way street.

I am also grateful to Philip Kowalski and Callie Garnett for help with illustrations.

I am also more grateful than I can say to Will Lippincott, who believed in this book from the start, and to George Gibson, my old-style hands-on editor, whose attentions have improved every page in this book. And I am grateful above all to Annie, who is the source of all the light I have.

Part I

Chapter 1

OMAR KHAYYAM AND HIS
RUBAIYAT

ONE DAY IN the summer of 1861 there appeared in a London bookstore's penny box a small paperbound volume of old Persian quatrains—called *rubaiyat* in Persian— attributed to the eleventh-century astronomer-mathematician- poet Omar Khayyam, and rendered into English by an anonymous Victorian writer later revealed to be one Edward FitzGerald. This slender volume, a pamphlet really, which had been published in 1859, but which had not sold or been read, was to have more success than any volume of poetry ever published in English. It begins,

> *Awake! For Morning in the Bowl of Night*
> *Has flung the Stone that puts the Stars to Flight:*
> *And Lo! The Hunter of the East has caught*
> *The Sultan's Turret in a Noose of Light.*

One of the first influential readers of Edward FitzGerald's *Rubaiyat of Omar Khayyam* was the Victorian art critic John Ruskin, who sat down in 1863 and wrote a short note to the author/translator whose name did not appear anywhere in the book. "My dear and very dear Sir," Ruskin wrote. "I do not know in the least who you are, but I do with all my soul pray you to find and translate some more of Omar Khayyam for us. I never did—til this day—read anything so glorious, to my mind, as this poem."

Ruskin's enthusiasm for FitzGerald's poems and a parallel enthusiasm for the eleventh-century Persian originals on which FitzGerald's work is based have multiplied a thousand-fold in the past 150 years. By 1929, there were 586 English editions of FitzGerald's poem. It has been translated into at least 54 languages. Khayyam's Persian quatrains (*ruba'i* is Persian for quatrain, *rubaiyat* is the plural) and FitzGerald's English translation/adaptation/ assembly interest people otherwise uninterested in poetry, even as the literary establishment continues to ignore his work. There are a few notable exceptions. Ezra Pound wrote in a letter "FitzGerald's trans. of Omar is the only good poem of the Vict. Era." Pound named his son Omar Shakespear Pound. T. S. Eliot came upon the *Rubaiyat* when he was still a boy. "I can recall clearly the moment," Eliot wrote years later. The effect of the *Rubaiyat* on the young Robert Bly was overwhelming. Bly was driving a tractor on the family farm in Madison, Minnesota, and reading the *Rubaiyat*. "He got so lost in the poetry he turned the tractor over."[1]

The Persian originals and their Victorian English versions offer a modern reader an accessible, appealing, sensuous, and above all a Lucretian or Epicurean worldview, an outlook based on respect for nature and a principled resistance to the consolations of organized religion. The *Rubaiyat* is exotic and familiar at the same time. Originally written in Farsi, Khayyam's separate and unrelated quatrains, of which many hundreds have survived, are a great if sometimes neglected achievement of the last phase of the Golden Age of Islam—the eighth through the middle of the eleventh century C.E.—an era of astonishing intellectual and artistic achievement in the Middle East at a time when the barbarian West was still sunk in the Dark Ages. Reading FitzGerald's *Rubaiyat* today suggests that there may be an alternative to the "clash of civilizations" idea that the culturally Christian West and the culturally Islamic Middle East are doomed to endless conflict.

What Omar's quatrains and FitzGerald's English versions seem to demonstrate is that just as Nishapur (Omar's birthplace and the site of his tomb) is a crossroads city on the old Silk Road (and the only city which the north and south Silk Road routes had in common) so Omar's and FitzGerald's poems lie at the intersection of medieval and modern, as well as at the intersection of East and West, at the very crossroads between Christian and Islamic civilization. The long continued interest in the *Rubaiyat*, both in the East and in the West, suggests that instead of an inevitable clash, there again could be, as there has already been, within limits, an attainable but not yet attained *convivencia* or *convivium,* a way to live together.

FitzGerald's *Rubaiyat* and the Persian quatrains from which FitzGerald's masterpiece was built are urban poetry, city poetry, as far from Jeffersonian or Wordsworthian ideals of the self-sufficient farmer and the wonders of nature as it is possible to get. In FitzGerald's rendering, the quatrains are also anti-Victorian and anti-Calvinist. Omar's medieval Persian work and FitzGerald's interest in it also illustrate just the opposite of Henri Pirenne's famous thesis, which was that the advent of Islam pushed the West into the Dark Ages. What actually happened was that the Dark Ages witnessed a growing knowledge in the West of Islam and its achievements in philosophy, medicine, and mathematics, knowledge that paved the way for the Western recovery of the classics and the Renaissance of learning.

FitzGerald's *Rubaiyat* is one of the great translations in world literature, on a par with the Baudelaire and Mallarmé translations of Edgar Allan Poe, the Schlegel-Tieck translations of Shakespeare, and the King James translation of the Bible. FitzGerald's work is also, importantly, a major case of reverse orientalism. Orientalism is the name given to a Western interest in Asian exoticism that subtly or not so subtly emphasizes the superiority of the rational West over the sensual East. FitzGerald's *Rubaiyat* points unmistakably to the poetic and philosophic superiority of eleventh-century Persia over the prosaic, superstitious, intellectually primitive eleventh-century West, a West still sunk in poverty, overrun by barbarians, confused, illiterate, depopulated, and primarily rural.[2] Far from looking down on Omar and his world, FitzGerald found there a better, more humane, more appealing world than that offered by Victorian England.

In FitzGerald's hands, individual Persian quatrains coalesced into one of the most moving and most often cited modern poetic statements about loss, longing, and nostalgia. The imagery of the *Rubaiyat* is wild, colorful, and memorable. It is a proto-modern achievement, hanging just on the lip of modernity. The *Rubaiyat*'s opening image is comparable in boldness and originality to the opening image of T. S. Eliot's "The

Love Song of J. Alfred Prufrock." The *Rubaiyat* opens with the lines quoted at the start of this chapter:

Awake! For Morning in the Bowl of Night
Has flung the Stone that puts the Stars to Flight:

Eliot's opening image in "Prufrock" could be the evening of Omar's day:

Let us go then, you and I,
When the evening is spread out against the sky
Like a patient etherized upon a table;

And just look at the bravado and the Yeatsian passion of the quatrain that is third from the end in all editions of the *Rubaiyat*:

Ah love! Could you and I with Fate conspire
To grasp this sorry Scheme of Things entire,
*   Would we not shatter it to bits and then*
Re-mould it nearer to the Heart's Desire!

———

It is a long way from Omar Khayyam to Edward FitzGerald, from eleventh-century Persia to nineteenth-century England, and FitzGerald's transformation of the Persian originals has an almost miraculous poetic quality. Here, for example, is a literal translation of one Persian quatrain in the Oxford manuscript that was FitzGerald's chief source.

Since no one can Tomorrow guarantee,
Enjoy the moment, let your heart be free;
   Ah, drink, my Moon, in moonlight for the moon
Will make its rounds but won't find you and me.[3]

And here, for comparison, is what FitzGerald made of the above, expanding one epigram into two and using them to end his English volume.

Ah, Moon of my Delight, who know'st no wane,
The Moon of Heav'n is rising once again
   How oft hereafter rising shall she look
Through this same Garden after me—in vain!

And when Thyself with shining Foot shall pass
Among the Guests Star-scatter'd on the Grass,
   And in thy joyous Errand reach the Spot
Where I made one—turn down an empty glass!

Who was Omar Khayyam? What was his Persia like? Who was Edward FitzGerald, and how did he come to reanimate the old Persian poems in modern England? How do we explain the quiet thunderbolt of a translation that is also a poetic master-piece? The story of the Rubaiyat is a silk road of the mind, a travel adventure of thought and poetry, that allows us to connect, personally, eleventh-century Persia and our own modern world.

Omar Khayyam

Chapter 2

THE LEGEND OF THE THREE STUDENTS

For some we loved, the loveliest and the best
That from his Vintage rolling Time hath prest,
Have drunk their Cup a Round or two before
And one by one crept silently to Rest.

O F THE HISTORICAL Omar Khayyam himself we know only a little, but, as with Shakespeare, we can infer quite a lot from that little. To make it more complicated, the sands of time have drifted over the real eleventh-century Persian astronomer-poet and his times, leaving us with myths and legends that, of course, contain their own kind of truths—important kinds—which must be excavated and understood as must the historical Omar and his actual circle of friends and associates.

The most enduring of the legends, the one FitzGerald did so much to spread, is the story of the three students of Nishapur. In the northeast corner of Persia—now Iran—in the capital city of the province of Khorasan, the city of Nishapur, there once lived three students. This was during the eleventh century as

Christians reckon, the fifth century as Muslims reckon. The three students all had the same teacher, the imam Mowaffak, who specialized in teaching the children of Nishapur's nobility. It was thought that anyone taught by Mowaffak would rise in the world, so one day the three students, figuring that at least one of them would succeed, made a pact that any one of the three who did succeed would share his good fortune with the other two. One of the students, Nizam al-Mulk, later became the most powerful man in Persia, vizier to the sultan himself. The second schoolfellow, Hasan-i Sabbah, later became the undisputed leader of a secret Shi'ite sect known as the Persian Ismailis, a sect or cult opposed to the Sunni sultan and his Sunni vizier, a sect centered in an impregnable fortress called Alamut located in the mountains northwest of present-day Tehran. Its modus operandi was targeted political assassination carried out by individual suicidal volunteers popularly supposed to be under the influence of hashish, hence called Hashishin or, as we now have it, assassins. Hasan's Khorasan based Assassins spread terror far and wide.

The third student, the son of a local tentmaker, was Omar (or, more usual now, Umar) Khayyam, who later became a noted philosopher, mathematician, astronomer, and, of course, poet. As the story has it, Nizam al-Mulk was the first to succeed, becoming as he did the vizier to the sultan Alp Arslan and then to Alp Arslan's son, Malik-Shah. Nizam did indeed share his good fortune. He gave Hasan a high place in the government and he offered the same to Omar. But Omar asked for a grant rather than a job, and Nizam obliged with a yearly stipend of 1,200 mithkals of gold, a Persian genius grant, worth, if we can believe the amount mentioned in the story, about $270,000 a year in current money.

This story was given wide circulation by FitzGerald, who told it at length in the introduction to his *Rubaiyat of Omar Khayyam*. The effect of the story has been to link the original poet of the *Rubaiyat* with some of the greatest men and events of his time, to suggest that the poet himself was a central figure in his time, and to encourage modern readers to look in Omar's poetry for hints about life, love, literature, and learning as they were experienced at the very center of Greater Persia during its finest time, the last phase of the Golden Age of Islam. The story of the three students has catapulted Omar Khayyam and his work onto a world stage.

But there are problems with the story. Nizam al-Mulk seems to have been born thirty years before Omar and Hasan; perhaps one of Nizam's many sons was one of the three, or perhaps it was Anushirwan bin Khalid, a later and lesser minister to a lesser sultan, but a man who was born at the same time and in the same city as Hasan.[1] Historical quibbling aside, though, what the story of the three students suggests, and what is perfectly true, is that Omar Khayyam's life and work, his quatrains and equations both, intersected with the lives and times of several of the major figures of his time and place. Omar's life *was* intimately connected with that of Nizam al-Mulk, the most powerful man, the prime minister of Seljuq Persia when it extended from the Mediterranean to China. Omar's life was also connected with the dark life of Hasan-i Sabbah, the grand master of the sect of the Assassins, the widely feared terrorist mastermind of the time. And that is not all.

Though the legend makes no mention of it, Omar's life was also intertwined with that of Abu Hamid al-Ghazali, often considered the most influential theologian of medieval Islam. Since Nizam al-Mulk, Hasan-i Sabbah, and Abu Hamid al-Ghazali were real people, not just figures in a legend, and since their ideas, their actions, and even their personalities show up repeatedly in quatrains of Omar's that were eventually taken up by FitzGerald, we can go back across time, along the silk road of poetry, to pick up what is known about these men and their era.

Chapter 3

THE WORLD OF OMAR KHAYYAM: NISHAPUR, KHORASAN, AND SELJUQ PERSIA

THE CHIEF SETTING for the life of Omar Khayyam and his friends was the city of Nishapur, the capital city of the province of Khorasan, a province the size of Germany located in the northeast of what is now Iran, but was then Persia. Nishapur was a large and important place in the eleventh century, with half a million or more inhabitants and a central position on the main east-west trade route, the great Silk Road itself. Eleventh-century Nishapur surpassed Baghdad and rivaled Constantinople in importance.

Nishapur was a walled city full of mosques, madrasas, markets, palaces, and gardens. Water flowed to gardens and courts from sources many miles away through carefully constructed stone-lined underground aqueducts called *qanats*. The city had Christian and Jewish quarters as well as quarters distinguished by trades and by tribes. Each quarter had its own market or bazaar as well as its own walls and gates, which it could close off in troubled times. Nishapur was known for its pottery (pots and pottery figure prominently in Omar's quatrains, where the Creator is the master potter whose creations not only hold water—and wine—but talk back), for turquoise from nearby mines, for fine cloth, and for an edible clay called *tin najahi*, much prized by gourmets. Carpets were woven in large workshops that worked on court commissions or for export. The narrow streets were also filled with students. Nishapur boasted some twenty-seven madrasas, religious schools, each with its own large building, classrooms, and library. In a madrasa schoolroom, the learned teacher would be seated in front of a crowd of students, each teacher flanked by two teaching assistants to help with explanation and commentary.

Nishapur was noted for its wealth and health and also for its fruit tree breeding and cultivation. In the walled gardens and in the farms and oases outside the city all kinds of fruit and vegetables grew under careful water management. The roses and the grapevines so celebrated by Omar only flourished because of the water carried by the qanats. A qanat might surface into a pool as large as an acre, from which thirty or forty smaller open channels fanned out to water the entire garden, like an oasis. If the water failed or the qanat collapsed the garden would go back to desert.[1] But while the water flowed, there were lemons, oranges, bitter oranges, plums, pears, apples, pomegranates, mulberries, walnuts, almonds, and pistachios.

Nishapur was more than a garden city. Cloth weavers used locally produced saffron, madder, henna, and indigo for dyes. Sesame oil was more used than olive oil. Dozens of different kinds of melons grew and as many as a hundred different varieties of grapes were grown for the flourishing wine trade. Despite the Islamic ban on alcohol, wine drinking was widespread and it has never had a greater poet than Omar Khayyam.

Perplext no more with Human or Divine,
Tomorrow's tangle to the winds resign,
   And lose your fingers in the tresses of
The Cypress-slender Minister of Wine.²

What Edward Gibbon said of the Roman Empire in the second century C.E., that it "comprehended the fairest part of the earth, and the most civilized portion of mankind," might with slight adjustment be applied to the eleventh century in the province of Khorasan. The 125,000-square-mile province, the largest in Persia, included, in Omar's day, lands now part of Afghanistan, Turkmenistan and Uzbekistan; the chief cities besides Nishapur were Tus, Merv, Samarcand, Bukhara, Mashad, Herat, and Balkh. Western Khorasan, the area around Nishapur, was the granary of all of Iran, growing rice and other grains, cotton, tobacco, and a little opium. Khorasan means "land where the sun rises," and we may see a poetic salute to Khorasan in the opening quatrain of FitzGerald's *Rubaiyat*, where dawn comes and the sultan's turret is caught in a noose of morning light.

As well as being the granary of the whole Upper Middle East, Khorasan contained the crucial central routes of the Silk Road, which was for this reason also known as the Great Khorasan Road. Here all branches of the Silk Road met and used the same track between Baghdad and Nishapur before westbound traffic broke off with one branch leading north to Constantinople while southwest-bound caravans headed down for Egypt and North Africa and the interior of Africa. Eastbound traffic on the Silk Road likewise split after passing Nishapur, the northeast road leading to Bukhara and eventually to Xi'an, then called Chang'an, deep inside China, while southbound traders turned off for India and Indian Ocean ports. Nishapur was the central junction city.

Astonishing amounts and varieties of goods, a world of gold bars and coins, silver dirhams, and all kinds of merchandise poured along the great road. From China came silk brocades, lacquerware, porcelain, gold-tinted paper, and jade. To China went dates, saffron, and pistachios from Persia; frankincense, aloes, and myrrh from Somalia; sandalwood from India; and glass bottles from Egypt. From the Turks and Slavs came furs, slaves, and metals, especially weapons. From northern India came slaves, cashmere clothing, and perfumes such as musk from Tibet. Traders also carried soap, sulphur, silks, jewels, sable, leatherware, ornamental weapons, and watermelons packed in snow.

There was no wheeled traffic. Everything went by horse or by the large two-humped Bactrian camels. During Omar's lifetime the Seljuq rulers of Khorasan planned and built the first caravanserais, overnight stopping places along the main routes. Each caravanserai had an outer wall enclosing a rectangular space with a single easily defended entrance at one of the narrow ends. The larger caravanserais provided food and entertainment, the smaller ones just lodging and stables. The largest could hold thousands of men, horses, and camels. The caravanserais were placed thirty kilometers, one day's travel, apart, and they quickly caught the imaginations of travelers and writers. Omar himself uses the caravanserai as a metaphor for the shortness of life.

Think, in this batter'd Caravanserai
Whose portals are alternate Night and Day,
*   How Sultan after Sultan with his Pomp*
Abode his destined Hour and went his way.³

―――――

Omar Khayyam lived and wrote during the great years of
the Seljuq era in Persia. The Seljuqs deserve to be better known.
A modern writer notes that "the entry of the Seljuq Turks into
Western Asia in the second half of the eleventh century forms
one of the great epochs of world history. It added a third
nation, after the Arabs and Persians, to the dominant races of
Islam: it prolonged the life of the moribund Caliphate for
another two hundred years, it tore Asia Minor away from
Christendom and opened the path to the later Ottoman invasion of Europe, it allowed the orthodox [Sunni] Muslims to
crush the Ismailian [Shi'ite] heresy, and provoked in reprisal
the murderous activities of the Assassins: it put an end to the
political domination of the Arabs in the Near East and spread
the language and culture of Persia over a wide area from
Anatolia to Northern India, and by posing a grave threat to the
Christian Powers, it impelled the Latin West to undertake the
remarkable counter-offensive of the Crusades."⁴

Omar Khayyam's life coincided almost perfectly with the
high point of the Seljuq era in Persia. Khayyam was born
in Nishapur in 1048, some ten years after Tughril, the first
Seljuq, captured that city in 1038. Khayyam was sixteen when
Alp Arslan succeeded Tughril in 1064, becoming Sultan and
appointing Nizam al-Mulk his vizier. Omar would have been

twenty-four when Alp Arslan was killed by a prisoner in 1072 and was succeeded by his eighteen-year-old son, Malik-Shah, the third and greatest of the Seljuq sultans, a patron of learning, science, art, and literature at whose court Omar Khayyam became a familiar figure. The quatrains attributed to Omar came not from a lonely outsider or a cloistered observer, but from a celebrated, well-traveled, sought-after intellectual, a figure at court at the heart of the empire, a mathematician and an astronomer who was also a sometime companion and drinking buddy of the sultan's. The poet of the quatrains had seen it all.

Chapter 4

THE EARLY YEARS
OF OMAR KHAYYAM

Myself when young did eagerly frequent
Doctor and Saint, and heard great argument
  About it and about: but evermore
Came out by the same door where in I went.

With them the seed of Wisdom I did sow
And with mine own hand wrought to make it grow
  And this was all the Harvest that I reap'd—
I came like Water, and like Wind I go.[1]

ANY MODERN PORTRAIT of Omar Khayyam is going to be a little like Mark Twain's description of the dinosaur in the museum: half a dozen bones and a dozen barrels of plaster. There are very few unchallenged facts about Khayyam's life, but there are numerous stories in which we catch glimpses of his personality. Whether true or not, the stories show what people thought of the man. We also know a fair amount about his time and place, so it is still possible to see him in that world.

Khayyam was said to be "shy and sensitive, with a bad temper; an impatient man," with little interest in teaching but with a remarkable memory and considerable self-discipline. On two separate occasions, we are told, he traveled to another city where he was allowed to read a book but not to copy it. On each occasion he returned home and wrote out a near-perfect version from memory. As a boy of perhaps twelve he is said to have asked his first teacher, one Imam Mawlana Qadi Muhammed, why, if it was the word of God, each chapter of the Qur'an begins "In the name of God, most merciful, most compassionate." Why does Allah refer to himself? Other stories show a similar unconventional directness, a person whose reported sayings are bold, straightforward, and tart, with wicked slivers of irony or wit. Asked to comment on a certain learned scholar's opposition to the work of Avicenna—a man revered by Khayyam—Khayyam sniffed, "Abu'l Barakat does not even understand the sense of the words in Avicenna; how can he oppose what he does not know?"[2]

Omar, or Umar, was born in 1048 in Nishapur. His father, Ibrahim, a tentmaker—*khayyam* means tentmaker—may have been a convert from Zoroastrianism to Sunni Islam. Most of Khorasan had been Zoroastrian before the Arab invasion of the mid-seventh century but only Sunni Muslims used the name Omar. The boy had the run of the old city, with its forty gated wards or quarters, its narrow streets, its mosques and minarets and madrasas. He would have known the markets and the workshops, the potters and the weavers, and he would have seen the merchants setting out for or coming in from their caravans on the Silk Road. A boy could not have asked for a busier,

more active, more colorful place in which to grow up. For not
only was Nishapur a lively commercial hub and meeting place,
it was also a city famous for its schools and its learning. There
were so many schools that a biographical dictionary was needed
just to name and list the thousands of students who passed
through the madrasas of Nishapur. Young Omar would have
seen streets filled with hundreds of students going to and from
their schools and tutors.

He himself was soon passed from Mawlana to another
teacher, Khawjah Abu'l Hasan al Anbari, with whom he studied
mathematics, astronomy, and cosmology, including, apparently,
Ptolemy's *Almagest,* a second-century-C.E. Greek treatise on
mathematical astronomy. From Anbari young Omar was passed
to Imam Mowaffak. Omar studied the Qur'an and jurispru-
dence with Mowaffak.

Mowaffak is the teacher in the story of the three students,
the story that misrepresents Nizam as Omar's schoolmate. Still,
the historical Nizam did figure, prominently, in Omar's later
life. In 1067, Nizam founded a new kind of madrasa, which
emphasized legal as well as religious learning. These new
schools, called Nizamiyahs, were started at Baghdad and at
Nishapur, and were intended to build a bridge between the religious and the political culture of Persia. Omar Khayyam was
nineteen at the time, an active and able student, and it may have
been at the new madrasa that he first came to the attention of
Nizam al-Mulk.

Nizam was at that moment forty-nine years old and, as
vizier to Sultan Alp Arslan, the most powerful political figure
in Khorasan during its greatest age. Widely regarded as the

Sultan Alp Arslan

Machiavelli of his time, he is said to have remarked that "one obedient slave is better than three hundred sons; for the latter desire their father's death, the former long life for his master."[3] In theory all power was vested in the sultan, who was God's representative on earth. In practice, much of this power and authority was delegated to others. The vizier, though he could be dismissed by the sultan at will and without cause, was, while in office, almost equal in power. Nizam oversaw four crucial departments of government: the department of appointments and correspondence, the department of the treasury—all money coming in or going out—the department of oversight and audit, and the department of the military. Nizam was so important he was allowed to be seated in the presence of the caliph, the nominal religious leader of the Sunni Seljuq sultans who were Nizam's masters. The vizier's office was conducted with great pomp; a pole bearing his seal or motto was, for example, held in front of him during conversations. Nizam's own opinion of himself was very high. "Tell the Sultan," he once wrote, "if you have not realized that I am your co-equal in the work of ruling, then know that you have only attained to this power through my statesmanship and judgement . . . If I ever close up this inkstand, that royal power will topple."[4]

Nizam al-Mulk had a personal household of thousands of persons; he had a private army made up of his own slaves; he entertained lavishly, kept an open table, made generous gifts to madrasas and hospices, and handed out pensions and grants to the pious, the learned, and the poor. Nizam was so powerful, so skillful, and so successful that five of his twelve sons, two grandsons, and one great-grandson held the office of vizier under one or another of the Seljuq sultans who followed Malik-Shah.

Details on the connection between the promising young student and the second greatest man in the Seljuq empire are scarce, but clearly Omar would not have become a favorite at the Seljuq court and a member of the intellectual elite around Sultan Malik-Shah unless he had been introduced and backed and favored by Nizam. And it is curious and almost spooky to learn that Nizam's dying words—"Oh God, I am passing away in the hand of the wind"—seem to be echoed, imperfectly, as the last line of one of Omar's quatrains, quoted at the head of this chapter.

Modern Persian scholars sometimes complain that Edward FitzGerald, trying to keep the poetry within reach of the nineteenth-century English reader, soft-pedaled or underplayed Omar's contemporaneous Persian references. However, when Omar says *Sultan* we need to remember that he personally knew several, including Malik-Shah, son of Alp Arslan, and Sanjar, son of Malik-Shah. When he talks about religious disputes, we need to remember that he himself wrote on religious subjects, was a passionate and lifelong defender of Avicenna, and knew personally al-Ghazali and other theologians. And when Omar talks about rulers and worldly power and influence, a flesh-and-blood Nizam al-Mulk, not an abstraction, lies behind the words.

Chapter 5

OMAR KHAYYAM AND THE COURT
OF THE SELJUQS

IN THE YEAR 1070, when Omar Khayyam was twenty-two
years old, he made a journey to Samarcand, where he had a
connection through a local judge, Abu Tahir, and set to work
writing an algebraic treatise on cubic equations. Two things
stand out: his interest not in poetry but in mathematics, and the
large distance he traveled. Samarcand was some five hundred
miles north and east of Nishapur, well beyond the lands ruled
by the Seljuqs at this time. More interestingly, twenty-two-
year-old Omar seems to have been known to his contempor-
aries as a philosopher and mathematician, and not as a poet.
There is no reference to his verses until more than a hundred
years after his death. His career and his main energies were in
philosophy, mathematics, and astronomy. Early modern interest
in Omar was centered on his contributions to mathematics
until FitzGerald's work brought attention to the quatrains.[1]

That the young mathematician should travel so far to a city
on the eastern side of the Amu Darya—long called the Oxus
River in the West—for a commission shows that Omar was
already linked up to a much larger world than that of Nishapur.

Alp Arslan was the sultan not just of Khorasan but of Greater Persia from the Mediterranean to the Oxus in 1070. Nizam al-Mulk had been his vizier for six years, trusted so fully that once, when Alp received a letter complaining about the vizier, he handed Nizam the letter, saying, "if they are right in what they have written, repair your nature and mend your ways; and if they have lied then forgive them their slip."[2] The following year, 1071, the thirty-nine-year-old Alp Arslan defeated a large Byzantine army under Emperor Romanus Diogenes IV at Manzikert (present-day Malazgirt, in Turkey) and captured the emperor. The Seljuqs also conquered Jerusalem this same year, thus setting in motion the events that would lead to the First Crusade.

Alp Arslan was tall: he wore a very high hat, called a *kulah*, and it was said "that from the top of this kulah to the ends of his mustaches was a distance of two yards." Indeed, his mustaches were so long that he had to tie them up when he wished to shoot. He was proud of his archery, which was natural for a warrior and an active leader of the army, but it also proved his undoing. In 1072, at the age of forty, Alp Arslan was menaced by a prisoner with a knife in front of two thousand people. The feisty Sultan signaled his guards to stand back as he intended to shoot the prisoner himself. His foot slipped, he missed his shot, and the prisoner killed him.[3]

Alp Arslan's son Malik-Shah was in his late teens at the time of his father's death. The new sultan had "a fair face, a full stature, was broad shouldered and slightly inclined to be stout. He had full whiskers and was light skinned, with color in his cheeks. He squinted slightly out of habit, not for any real reason."[4]

He was good with weapons, a skilled rider, who both fought and played polo. He was nimble and quick and loved games.

As a ruler, Malik-Shah expanded Greater Persia until it reached from Kashgar in the east to the Bosphorus and the Mediterranean in the west, and from the Caucasus and the Aral Sea in the north to Yemen and the Indian Ocean. The new young sultan kept Nizam al-Mulk on as vizier, who at the age of fifty-five thus became the de facto co-ruler along with the eighteen-year-old Malik-Shah of an empire stretching from China to the Mediterranean.

Malik-Shah was not only the greatest of the Seljuqs, he was also a major patron of the arts, the sciences, and learning generally. In 1074, at age twenty-one, he established an observatory and launched a project to reform the calendar, summoning Omar Khayyam, then twenty-six years old, as one of a group of leading mathematicians and astronomers. For the next eighteen years or so, Omar was close to Malik-Shah and his court.

The Seljuq court was essentially a military court; much time and money was spent on the army and its campaigns. The troops were led by the sultan in person and the camp or court included women and children as well as soldiers. The court was not a fixed place, but was wherever the sultan himself happened to be. Malik-Shah's favorite city was Isfahan, where the new observatory was built and where Omar Khayyam went to work on the new calendar. The vizier, in charge of the treasury and so much else, went everywhere with the sultan. And his court included many bureaucrats, clerics, hostages, scholars, and poets. The civilian and military aspects of court life over-

Sultan Malik-Shah I

lapped. The polo master also oversaw the cavalry. The master of the kitchen was also the quartermaster. The size of the court can be glimpsed from the fact that Sultan Alp Arslan's standing order was for fifty sheep a day to be slaughtered.

The Seljuq court favored intellectuals and poets. Besides Omar Khayyam, Malik-Shah gathered to his court the philosopher and theologian Ghazali, the poet Mu'izzi, and the poet Sanai. Omar himself was even, according to one account, one of the sultan's "boon companions," a vacuous Victorianism for "drinking buddy."[5] Nizam himself, in his *Siyasat Nama* (*Book of Government or Rules for Kings*), written at the request of Malik-Shah in the late 1080s, described the role of the "boon companions." "It is only through his boon companions that the king's spirit is set free, and if he wants to live more fully, to refresh himself in sport and jest, to tell stories, jokes, and curious tales, he can enjoy these things without detriment to his majesty and sovereignty, because he keeps them for this very purpose."[6] Seljuq court life, the life Omar Khayyam knew, was in part modeled on the eighth-century Baghdad court of Haroun al-Rashid (Aaron the Upright), the sultan of the *Arabian Nights*. He had a common touch, walked barefoot through the mud to his mother's funeral, and preferred hunting lodges to Baghdad. Haroun was fond of disguises; he delighted in slipping out of the palace with a small band of loyal companions and mingling with ordinary people.

Omar Khayyam was favored and valued by Malik-Shah for his learning and his skill at mathematics, astronomy, and perhaps philosophy, but not for poetry. Malik-Shah's poet laureate was Mu'izzi, who followed his father in the position and had one of the qualities most valued in a court poet: improvisational skill and quickness. One night the court crowd came outdoors to look for the moon. The king, who emerged with his hunting bow in his hand, was the first to see it. One of the courtiers immediately turned to the poet and said, "Say something appropriate." Mu'izzi reported that he "at once recited" this quatrain or ruba'i;

> *Methinks O Moon thou art our prince's bow*
> *Or his arched eyebrow which doth charm us so*
> *Or else a horse-shoe wrought of gold refined*
> *Or ring from heaven's ear depending low.*

The quick-witted poet's reward was as quickly given. The king said, "Go, loose from the stables whichever horse thou pleasest." A little later the same day, Mu'izzi, challenged again, this time to comment on the gift, swiftly produced another ruba'i and the king gave him a thousand dinars.[7]

Omar's own attitude toward court life seems to have been quite different. For one thing, he took the long view:

Whether at Naishapur or Babylon
Whether the cup with sweet or bitter run,
*   The Wine of Life keeps oozing drop by drop,*
The Leaves of Life keep falling one by one.

And when Omar wrote about the moon, it came out quite differently than it did from Mu'izzi:

Yon rising Moon that looks for us again—
How oft hereafter shall she wax and wane;
*   How oft hereafter rising look for us*
Through this same Garden—and for one in vain!

Omar's real interests, as reflected in his quatrains, were about as far from the life of the court as can be imagined. In what has become his best-known quatrain, he clearly prefers a quiet picnic lunch for two in the countryside to the vast royal banquets the Seljuq sultans loved to give.

A Book of verses underneath the Bough
A Jug of Wine, a Loaf of bread—and Thou
*   Beside me in the Wilderness—*
Oh, Wilderness were Paradise enow![8]

No one knows when Omar Khayyam began to write the quatrains for which FitzGerald has made him so famous. They read, at first glance, like the work of an old, weary, unillusioned man who has seen everything and has come to understand the impermanence of life, the basic truth that nothing gold can stay. But look again. The poet doesn't dismiss or reject or brood over lost time and vanished youth. He loves it, celebrates it, knows it to be all the sweeter for being temporary. The quatrain just quoted is hardly the work of a burnt-out case. The lines could easily have been written by a very young poet, and they appeal with assured personal warmth to young adolescent readers, to first-time lovers in all languages and lands.

There are other reasons to think that some of the quatrains supposedly written by Omar Khayyam and translated so successfully by FitzGerald may have been written not by an old man but by a young, or at least a younger, man still immersed in the working world, the court world, the Persian world at the apex of Seljuq power and influence. If we accept Edward Heron-Allen's remark that the Omar Khayyam of the quatrains was a "transcendental agnostic and an ornamental pessimist," we may also note that young adults are the natural pessimists. Apprehensive that their lives and loves may not turn out to match their dreams, young people adopt the tragic view of life to explain potential failure. The poetry of pessimism, of Omar/ FitzGerald, Houseman, Eliot, Frost, and the rest, while it *seems* to give us the worldview of older people, actually gives us the young person's take on that world. Whether Omar's or FitzGerald's, the empty heaven merely confirms what one has long suspected. So too something about Omar's insistence on the futility of learning is comforting, just as there is something satisfying in youth's anticipatory nostalgia, the eager looking forward to the pleasures of looking backward. There is something sadly appealing, something pleasantly confirming about our visions of lost empires, ruined cities, and dethroned kings. It is the worldview of Ozymandias, and of the uncle who likes to say I told you so. Omar's conclusion? The same as Strethers' in *The Ambassadors*. Live all you can. Right now. It's a mistake not to.

Chapter 6

OMAR KHAYYAM AND HIS
ASSOCIATES, 1075–1090

THE YEARS FROM 1075 to 1090 mark the high point of the Seljuq empire, which was short-lived but glorious while it lasted. The same period marks the high point of Omar Khayyam's public life as a mathematician, astronomer, and philosopher, and it is also the period in which Khayyam's life is most interwoven with the lives of Nizam, Hasan-i Sabbah, and Abu Hamid al-Ghazali, interweavings that influenced the course of events in Persia and left footprints in the quatrains that, even if the rubaiyat are not all Omar's own, would nevertheless be collected and go down to posterity under Omar's name.

In 1075 Omar was twenty-seven and still living in Nishapur when he was asked by Nizam and Malik-Shah to travel to Isfahan to work on reforming the Islamic calendar. His old school friend Hasan had, according to legend, a position in the government, thanks also to Nizam. But Hasan, the future grand master of the Assassins of Alamut, having tried to set Malik-Shah against Nizam, had been found out and chased from court.

Hasan self-identified as Arab, not as Persian and certainly not as Turkish; his father, who came from Yemen, was said to be of Arab descent. Hasan was probably born in Qum—or Qom, as it is commonly transliterated now—a Shi'ite town in western Iran. He studied in Rayy, now a suburb of Tehran, where he met one Amira Dharrab who introduced him to the radical branch of Shi'ism whose followers were called Ismailis. Shi'ites believe that the prophet Muhammed's authority was passed directly and personally from Ali, Muhammed's nephew and son–in law (married to Fatima, the prophet's daughter). Sunni Muslims believe that Muhammed's authority was originally passed on by consensus of the group of companions around the prophet. Authority for a Shi'ite is personal, passed from one family member to the next of kin, the next in line. Authority for a Sunni is something determined by the community of believers, persons attached to the prophet not by blood but by like-mindedness. Hasan spent his adult life fighting against the Sunni establishment in Persia presided over by Malik-Shah and Nizam, both of whom Hasan openly despised, referring once to them as "this Turk and this peasant." He also once said that "the Turks were jinn, not men."[1]

In 1075, after being thrown out of Malik-Shah's court, Hasan went to the city of Isfahan, where Omar appeared the next year. Hasan was overheard by his host or landlord complaining about Nizam and Malik-Shah and saying, "Ah, if only I had two faithful and devoted friends, I would soon be delivered." Hasan's host was no fool. He treated this homicidal hint as proof that Hasan was crazy, so every day he mixed a remedy against dementia into Hasan's food. Hasan caught on to this and left the house never to return.

Drawn to moral rigor, and to a pitiless, intense, and severe logic, Hasan later sent his daughters away with their mother to spin yarn at a distant place from which he did not bring them back. He had both his sons executed, one for murder (the charge is said to have proved false), the other for drinking wine, which is forbidden to strictly observant Muslims. Once when some of his followers presented him with a genealogy produced as an elegant book, Hasan is said to have tossed it in a pool of water, remarking that he would rather be an imam's favored servant than his degenerate son.[2] Hasan nursed his hatred of Nizam through the 1070s and '80s to a disastrous conclusion. If Omar had any direct dealings with Hasan during these years, we do not know about them. But Omar would have had ample motivation for avoiding the smoldering Hasan, who was already well on his way to becoming an archetype of religious/political villainy, a rigid and difficult man with his virulent and violent antiestablishment version of Shi'ism. Hasan would have despised any of Omar's quatrains he might have come across. Omar's preference for wine over logic, and for love over power, could only have stirred Hasan's contempt. There is no possibility that the puritanical Hasan, school friend of Omar's or not, would have been able to tolerate such lines as these, expressing, as they do, the doubt and disobedience common in quatrains attributed to Omar Khayyam:

> *What, without asking, hither hurried Whence?*
> *And, without asking, Whither hurried hence!*
> *Oh, many a Cup of this forbidden Wine*
> *Must drown the memory of that insolence!*

———

In 1077, the twenty-nine-year-old Omar, still in Isfahan, and still working on calendar reform for the sultan, finished work on a commentary on Euclid's theory of parallel lines and theory of ratios. Also this year, a nineteen-year-old named Abu Hamid al-Ghazali, a man destined to become a great theologian and philosopher, enrolled as a student at the Nizamaya madrasa in Nishapur. Ghazali would remain in Nishapur for the next eight years and become a student of Omar Khayyam's. Embarrassed to be seen going to the home of a man who was beginning to be suspected as a freethinker (perhaps a few quatrains had begun to leak out), young Ghazali tried to arrive and depart from Khayyam's house without being seen. Khayyam is said to have hired a drummer to stand on the roof and beat his drum to advertise Ghazali's approach.

Ghazali would rise to fill the most important teaching post in the Islamic world of his time and place, the directorship of the Nizamaya madrasa in Baghdad, and he wrote many treatises against Hasan's Ismailis. He also worked out a theory reconciling religious and political leadership, an arrangement by which the caliph—supreme in religious matters—and the sultan—supreme in secular matters—could work together. And in the mid-1090s, after a personal crisis, a withdrawal from office and public life, and a rethinking of everything, Ghazali reconstructed his new life on a thoroughly Sufi basis, a way of thinking and living that Omar would also find compelling.

———

From 1078 to 1080, Hasan-i Sabbah was in Cairo, at the Fatimid court, the epicenter of the Ismaili Shi'ite world. He seems to have been drawn to controversy and trouble like a moth to a flame. During Hasan's time in Egypt, the Egyptian army's senior general persuaded Caliph Mostansir to disinherit his—the caliph's—son Nizar and appoint another son, Mosta'li, his successor. (Mosta'li just happened to be the general's godson.) Hasan publically backed Nizar, but the general got his way and Hasan was promptly expelled from the country. Hasan then returned to Khorasan, where he organized the underground Nizari-Ismailian-Shi'ite revolutionary movement, a nation within a nation that was to have, in a few short years' time, disruptive, disastrous results for the Seljuqs, for Nizam, and for Omar Khayyam.

In 1079, the new calendar Omar had worked on for four years was introduced on March 15, in the Year of the Hegira 471, inaugurating what Malik-Shah announced as the Jalalian Era. Omar had written a history (which has not survived) of previous calendar reform. He and his colleagues then produced a new calendar based on their calculation of the solar year as 365.2424 days, and starting the new year at the vernal equinox. Omar's calendar, a version of which is still in use in Iran, is a little more accurate than the Gregorian calendar, which is still in wide use in most of the world. The superiority of Omar's calendar is its calculation of the solar year. The Gregorian calendar assumes the solar year to be 365.2425 days, so the Gregorian calendar needs a makeup day every 3,333 years, while Omar's needs a makeup day every 5,000 years.[3]

With the calendar work completed, Omar returned to Nishapur, where around 1083 he was engaged in writing a treatise in philosophy, on the general subject of Being and Necessity.

What survives of this work on the nature of reality is philosophical hardball. "There is no being about which 'whether it exists' cannot be asked, and what is devoid of 'I-ness' and verifiability is nonexistent," Omar wrote, with a great deal more just like it.[4] Long before Sartre, the Persian Omar was immersed in Being and Nothingness. For it is not just the philosophical treatise but the quatrains that make the point over and over that there is nothing we can't ask about, though we may not like the answers.

A Moment's Halt—a momentary taste
Of BEING from the Well amid the Waste—
And Lo!—the phantom Caravan has reach'd
The NOTHING it set out from—Oh, make haste!

If this is nihilism, it is a genial and affirmative nihilism. The transient present—what William James would call the specious present (a period of about twelve seconds which we *feel* to be not past or future but present)—is all the more valuable when one realizes it is all there is, and all there is going to be. Both the Persian original quatrains and FitzGerald's gorgeous versions gleam with what George Santayana called intellectual anarchy, a consciousness which, however confused, "is full of light; its blindness is made up of dazzling survivals, revivals and fresh beginnings. Were it not for these remnants or seeds of order, chaos itself could not exist; it would be nothing." A significant part of the appeal of the quatrains attributed to Omar and redelivered by FitzGerald lies in their open and emotional directness, their Shakespearian

directness, about our all-too-common misgivings about what
is really real.

> *Ah, make the most of what we yet may spend,*
> *Before we too into the Dust descend;*
> *Dust into Dust, and under Dust to lie,*
> *Sans Wine, sans Song, sans Singer, and—sans End!*

Chapter 7

THE DISASTROUS DECADE:
THE 1090S

A SERIES OF CALAMITOUS events in the first half of the decade of the 1090s brought an end to the great years of the Seljuqs in Iran, brought chaos and instability more widely to the Islamic lands and peoples of the Middle East, and utterly changed the lives of Ghazali and Omar Khayyam and many others. The first of these events was Hasan-i Sabbah's seizure of the fortress of Alamut high in the Elburz mountains about seventy miles northwest of modern-day Tehran. Only a few miles south of the Caspian Sea, Alamut was an essentially impregnable mountaintop stronghold whose sides were too steep to assault. It was approachable only by an easily defended narrow winding road that crossed several chasms. Hasan seized the place by guile on the night of September 4, 1090, and quickly made it the center of the Nizari Ismaili Shi'ite rebellion in Iran. From the castle of Alamut Hasan was soon dispatching individual assassins on suicide missions, carefully targeted public murders intended to terrorize and undermine the Sunni Seljuq establishment. Hasan and Alamut (which means Eagle's Nest) quickly attracted stories too lurid to be strictly true but expressive nevertheless of what people of the time were willing to believe about the Assassins and their chief. The most colorful and enduring stories about Alamut come from the Venetian Marco Polo who visited Alamut some fifteen years after the fortress was destroyed in 1256 by Hulagu Khan, the grandson of Genghis Khan. In breathless goggle-eyed prose, Polo told how Hasan, whom he called the Old Man of the Mountains, created a Potemkin paradise at Alamut, a walled mountain pleasure-palace garden with running water, fruit trees, and unlimited sweet desserts and wine served by attractive and approachable girls in gossamer silks. The Old Man, in Polo's account, when he wanted a volunteer for an assassination would summon a young man, give him a drug, and let him wake up in the garden and find his wildest dreams fulfilled. The

Site of the fortress of Alamut

young man would then be drugged again and would be removed from the paradaisical playground, taken before the Old Man, and dispatched on his mission to kill, with the promise of a sure return (alive or dead) to Paradise upon completion.

How soon after Hasan's seizing of Alamut in 1090 such stories began to circulate cannot be determined, but the vision of paradise in Khayyam's quatrains amounts to a deliberate rejection of the fantasy bordello of Hasan's Alamut. Instead of a cynical political paradise in which a crowd of houri-like maidens manipulates a steady stream of eager young killers, Omar finds Paradise where any two lovers meet. A literal translation of one of the quatrains FitzGerald translated makes the point emphatically.

> *I desire a flask of ruby wine and a book of verses*
> *Just enough to keep me alive, and half a loaf is needful,*
>   *And then, that thou and I should sit in the wilderness,*
> *Is better than the kingdom of a Sultan.*[1]

The historical Hasan seems to have relied more on logic and persuasion than on charades to maintain his position and bring in recruits. Hasan even seems to have become a sort of place-holder for the next (but unknown, unrevealed at the time) Shi'ite Nizari Ismaili caliph, and he developed a rigorous logical argument that served to justify his remorseless despotism. It was an elaborate defense of the Ismaili version of the Shi'ite conviction that religious authority had necessarily to reside exclusively in one infallible imam at a time. Hasan's position was clever, logical—dialectical in fact—and narrow. His first proposition was "that for the absolute truth about God, either one needs a teacher to know God or not; but if not, then one cannot prefer one's own speculation to another's—for the denial of another's views is an implicit teaching of him." Therefore one needs a teacher.[2]

Hasan's second proposition was "either the teacher must be authoritative or any teacher will do." But the latter alternative "leads us back where we were to start with—it gives no basis for supporting one teacher against another." So the teacher must be authoritative.

Hasan's third proposition was the crucial one. "Either the authority of the teacher must be demonstrated or, any teacher must be accepted as authoritative." As before, the second alternative leads nowhere and leaves no ground for choice. But the first alternative poses a problem. How can the one absolutely authoritative imam demonstrate his absolute authority without invoking some further authority for the demonstration? Hasan's answer was this: "Without the Imam, reason leads to a blank wall. Without reason, the Imam rests unproven, and so unknown."

In his fourth proposition Hasan put these two statements together; so "the only true Imam must be that Imam who depends on this [very] dialectical process [we are discussing] for his demonstration. Any Imam who seeks a proof in lineage or in miracles or what-not is obviously a pseudo imam." As an argument it greatly irritated both Ghazali and Omar Khayyam. Everything we know about Hasan suggests he believed in a rigid monolithic absolutism and authoritarianism. He was cold, hard, and unpleasant, a Dickensian villain. There can only be one truth and one leader. The one leader was Hasan-i Sabbah; the one truth was his truth. Everything and everyone else was subordinate or wrong.

Ghazali made a formal, reasoned response to Hasan's argument, saying in effect that not only could reason establish the need for an authority beyond reason, reason could also recognize—could *begin* to recognize—when that need had been fulfilled. Ghazali further argued that the "true Imam was none but the Prophet himself, whose teaching would be found valid in each person's life."[3] Omar Khayyam also replied to Hasan's logic, but *his* reply was to mock it.

> For "*is*" and "*is-not*" though with Rule and Line
> And "*up-and-down*" by logic I define,
>   Of all that one should care to fathom, I
> Was never deep in anything but wine.

For Omar wine was not the problem, as it was for Hasan; it was the solution. Omar salutes "the grape that can with logic absolute/ The two-and-seventy jarring sects confute." (The prophet Muhammed had said his community would eventually split into seventy-two different sects.) Omar, like the later Ghazali, thought real religion was an individual matter, which institutions might or might not help:

> And this I know: whether the one True Light
> Kindle to Love, or Wrath-consume me quite,
>   One Flash of It within the Tavern caught
> Better than in the Temple lost outright.

In 1092, two years after Hasan seized Alamut, one of his assassins, dressed as a Sufi but armed with a sword, struck down and killed the seventy-four-year-old vizier Nizam al-Mulk at Sihna, a place on the road between Isfahan and Baghdad. Nizam had been on his way to Mecca; he was killed on the tenth day of the Islamic holy month of Ramadan. Dying, the old man cried out, "Oh God, I am passing away in the hand of the wind." It is a little eerie then, to find among the quatrains attributed to Omar this one with its backward glance and its apparent echo, given here not in FitzGerald's version but in Heron-Allen's more literal translation:

> For a while, when young, we frequented a teacher,
> For a while we were contented with our proficiency;
> Behold the end of the discourse: what happened to us?
> We came like water and we went like wind.[4]

Less than a month after Hasan's assassin had felled Nizam, the sultan Malik-Shah, who was only thirty-eight, died of complications arising from a cold caught while out hunting. Omar Khayyam had been a favorite of both Nizam and Malik-Shah, but he was not in favor with those who now took over. Malik-Shah's widow, regent for four-year-old Sultan Mahmud, did not approve of Omar, and others at court disliked the religious views expressed in quatrains attributed to him. Omar seems to have immediately grasped the seriousness of his newly precarious position. On his way to Bukhara when the news of Malik-Shah's death reached him late in the year 1092, Omar changed course at once and started to make his own self-protective pilgrimage to Mecca. Many of Omar's quatrains speak of change and of uncertainty about the future; it is not possible to date them with accuracy, but such quatrains are poignant expressions of change and its repercussions and could easily have been written with the early 1090s in mind.

> *Indeed the Idols I have loved so long*
> *Have done my credit in this World much wrong:*
> *Have drown'd my glory in a shallow Cup*
> *And sold my reputation for a Song.*

One quatrain seems especially apt for a forty-four-year-old man facing a time of drastic and unwelcome changes.

> *Yet Ah, that Spring should vanish with the Rose!*
> *That Youth's sweet scented manuscript should close!*
> *The Nightingale that in the branches sang,*
> *Ah whence, and whither flown again who knows?*

These are very general, to be sure, but some darker quatrains contain references to the Angel of Death and to "the dark Ferrash," the executioner, quatrains that seem aimed at Hasan himself:

> *So when that Angel of the darker Drink*
> *At last shall find you by the river-brink,*
> *And, offering his Cup, invite your Soul*
> *Forth to your Lips to quaff—you shall not shrink.*

Grimmest of all is one in which the tent is an image of the short-lived body.

> 'Tis but a Tent where takes his one day's rest
> A Sultan to the realm of death addrest;
>   The Sultan rises, and the dark Ferrash
> Strikes, and prepares it for another Guest.[5]

Chapter 8

THE SUFI TURN

IF MANY OF Omar's quatrains can be read as responses to the extremist views and actions of Hasan and his Ismaili followers, virtually all of Omar's quatrains can be—and have been—read as endorsements of a quite different religious outlook, that of Sufism. The inner, mystical dimension of Islam, Sufism is a way of thinking and living that has some elements of what is sometimes called the perennial philosophy. Sufis believe that the individual can draw closer to God and embrace the divine presence experientially in *this* life. Nizam al-Mulk had been a great protector of the Sufis, the Seljuqs embraced them, and indeed it was during the Seljuq era that Sufism found its way, in a modified form, into Sunni orthodoxy itself.[1]

When, in 1095, Abu Hamid al-Ghazali underwent a personal crisis and left his prestigious post at Baghdad to retire and rethink his life and his work, it was because he had come to doubt all the religious views he had been teaching and had come to feel "he could be healed only by accepting a moral decision to withdraw and lay new bases for his life through Sufi practices."[2] Ghazali's new orientation appeared most clearly in

1106 when he resumed teaching under the protection of one of Nizam's sons, not at Baghdad, but back in Nishapur.

Omar Khayyam had Sufi connections, if not roots. He had been personally acquainted with the first great Sufi poet, Sana'i of Ghazna, who had paid the twenty-seven-year-old Khayyam a visit in 1075 at Nishapur. While Khayyam knew Abu Hamid al-Ghazali, perhaps more importantly he knew his brother Ahmad Ghazali, who was a noted Sufi master. Ahmad Ghazali is even said to have commented on some of Omar's quatrains.

The idea that Omar was a Sufi gets strong support from such quatrains as this one:

> *I sent my Soul through the Invisible,*
> *Some letter of that After-life to spell:*
>   *And by and by my Soul return'd to me,*
> *And answer'd "I myself am Heav'n and Hell."*

The Sufic message is even stronger in the Persian original behind FitzGerald's lines. The Persian emphasizes the role of the teacher, a crucial part of the transmission of Sufi belief.

> *Already on the Day of Creation, beyond the heavens, my soul*
> *Searched for the Tablet and Pen, and for heaven and hell;*
> *At last the Teacher said to me with his enlightened judgment,*
> *Tablet and Pen, and heaven and hell, are within thyself.*[3]

As Sufism depends upon a kind of knowing and insight beyond mere rationalism, it is not hard to see a Sufi statement in a quatrain such as this:

You know, my Friends, with what a brave Carouse
I made a Second Marriage in my house;
Divorced old barren Reason from my Bed
And took the Daughter of the Vine to Spouse.

An extreme and relatively recent example of interpreting Omar Khayyam as a Sufi is Paramahansa Yogananda's reading of the second quatrain of FitzGerald's first edition:

Dreaming when Dawn's Left Hand was in the sky
I heard a Voice within the Tavern cry,
"Awake, my Little ones, and fill the Cup
Before Life's Liquor in its Cup be dry."

"Dawn's Left Hand" means, says Yogananda, "the perennial wisdom and the first yearning to solve the riddles of life." "A voice" means "intellectual intuition," and "tavern" is the "sanction of inner silence." "Fill the Cup" is "the consciousness of the mystic" and the "Cup" is "the corporeal body which needs to be filled with the new intellect."[4]

Whether or not one can accept the allegorical equivalences of Yogananda, there are solid reasons to believe that the historical Omar Khayyam had broad Sufi sympathies. The last treatise he is known to have written, composed around 1106, is called "On the Knowledge of the Universal Principles of Existence." The third section of this treatise contains an explicit endorsement of the Sufi way. After listing three other types of knowers, Khayyam says, "Fourth are the Sufis, who do not seek knowledge intellectually or discursively, but by the cleansing of their inner self and through purgation of their morals, they have cleansed their rational soul from the impurities of nature and incorporeal body . . . This path is the best of them all. For it becomes known to the servant of God that there is no perfection better than the presence of God, [in the soul] and in that state, there are no obstacles or veils. For all that man lacks is due to the impurities of nature, for if the [spiritual] veil is lifted and the screen and the obstacle is removed, the truth of things as they really are becomes apparent."[5]

Omar's quatrains themselves and his extraordinary and direct praise for the Sufi way show pretty clearly that Omar Khayyam, while not an avowed, formal, or practicing member of a Sufi order or brotherhood, nor yet a man with a proper Sufi master or teacher, was nevertheless broadly sympathetic to Sufi aims and methods and ideas. If not a card-carrying Sufi, he was certainly a fellow traveler. Sufism shares important ground with Jewish, Christian, Buddhist, and Hindu mysticism, and the presence of Sufism, permeating Omar Khayyam's poetry as it does, is one reason why that poetry has been and can be so widely appreciated and understood.

Chapter 9

OMAR KHAYYAM'S *RUBAIYAT*

SEEING OMAR KHAYYAM as a Sufi or Sufi sympathizer and reading his poetry through a Sufi lens in which everything is allegorized—wine is wisdom or love, drunkenness is devotion to God—also insulates him against charges of heresy, agnosticism, and hedonism. This has been especially true in Persian/Iranian culture, where, as the modern Khayyam scholar Mehdi Aminrazavi plainly puts it, "one is either a heretic or *somewhere* within the pale of religion. Khayyam could not have been the former, therefore he has to be the latter."[1] If he really was a Sufi or Sufi sympathizer, then we can brush past much of the contemporaneous judgment on him, judgment such as that pronounced by Daya, a thirteenth-century Persian writer, who said that while Khayyam was "famous for his talents, his wisdom, intelligence, and doctrine, he was also one of those unfortunate philosophers and materialists who, detached from divine blessings, wander in stupefaction and error."[2]

We don't know when Omar Khayyam began to write the quatrains that survive under his name. He could have been composing them all through his career. But because the earliest surviving manuscripts were written a hundred years after his death, often by anonymous scribes anxious not to be connected with a suspected freethinker, and because a good number of quatrains alleged to be by him have been shown to be the work of other poets, we cannot even say with certainty which of the hundreds of quatrains carrying his name were really composed by him. One of the best-known quatrains, best-known because FitzGerald included his version of it in his *Rubaiyat of Omar Khayyam*, has been shown to be by Avicenna.[3]

Medhi Aminrazavi's recent, wide-ranging, and authoritative account of Khayyam, *The Wine of Wisdom*, lists the sixteen oldest and most likely to be authentic quatrains.[4] Aminrazavi next gives a list of thirty-one quatrains that have been accepted as genuine by various modern Persian scholars. He further notes that the eminent Khayyam scholar Ali Furughi accepts as genuine one hundred and seventy-eight quatrains. But other manuscript collections contain many more quatrains, so that the total number attributed to Omar Khayyam is somewhere between twelve hundred and fourteen hundred. Despite heroic winnowing efforts, there is no rock-solid proof of his author-ship of any of them. Still, the fact that so many quatrains were gathered together under his name and not someone else's is a clear indication that Khayyam was generally known as a leading author of just the kind of skeptical, questioning, and bold quatrains that bear his name.

Besides the controversy over authorship, what remains, of course, are the quatrains themselves, and it is only because we do have the quatrains that we are even interested in the question of who wrote them. Several, perhaps many, poets sought shelter under Khayyam's large tent. It makes sense, then, even if we find the historical Khayyam a credible figure, to speak of something larger, of a Khayyamian school of thought and poetry, representing "the voices of those thinkers who for centuries have spoken through a proxy without being lynched by the orthodox."[5] The quatrains speak for themselves and they can be studied, for both form and content.

The ruba'i or quatrain is a Persian invention and the "oldest indigenous verse-form produced in Iran."[6] It has been compared to the limerick and to epigraphs such as those in the *Greek Anthology*, the influential fourteenth-century C.E. collection of classical Greek and Byzantine short poems and epitaphs. Each ruba'i is made up of two *bayt*s, a bayt being a two-line unit, and the basic unit of Persian poetry. Each four-line ruba'i is self-contained, and the first, second, and fourth line must rhyme. The meter has a swing to it, but is, says the literary historian E. G. Browne, "next door to impossible to imitate in English." The last line of each quatrain springs the trap, makes the leap, flips the subject on its back, completing the quatrain with an extra dash of energy or wit. It has been well said that a successful ruba'i is like a discrete thing that keeps its mystery, such as a seed, a flower, a constellation of stars. Persian rubaiyat are not strung together to tell a story, so there are no ruba'i sequences such as the sonnet sequences so frequent in English poetry. Collections of Persian rubaiyat, which are common enough, are always organized only alphabetically, according to the last letter of the rhyme word in each quatrain.

The window through which Omar Khayyam's quatrains

came to wide modern attention is the manuscript that so deeply impressed Edward FitzGerald when he saw it in the 1850s. It was then and is now in Oxford's Bodleian library, where it was known as Ouseley Manuscript 140 though it is now listed as Bodleian MS 140. Sir William Ouseley was a British diplomat who spent time in Persia and collected hundreds of manuscripts. This one measures less than three inches by six and is written in Farsi in the beautiful cursive script called Nasta'lik, on thick yellow paper in black-purple ink profusely powdered with gold. It was created in Shiraz in 1460 by one Mahmud Yerbudaki three hundred and thirty-odd years after Khayyam's death. No manuscript in Khayyam's own hand or from his own time has yet been found. The Ouseley manuscript is not inherently more authoritative than other manuscripts. It is important mainly because it was the first and most important manuscript for FitzGerald. Ouseley 140 contains 158 quatrains, and even a quick look at them can still give one some feeling for the quatrains of Omar before FitzGerald got to him. The manuscript opens with a little theological protest:

> *If I have never threaded the pearl of thy service*
> *I have, at least, never wiped the dust of sin from my face;*
> *This being so, I am not hopeless of Thy mercy,*
> *For the reason that I have never said that One was Two.*[7]

"To thread pearls" is a Persian locution for writing verses or telling a story. The last line is a claim that the poet has never questioned the unity of God. This, and the quatrains that follow in this chapter, are the plain translations of Edward

Heron-Allen, who set out to give English readers a solid literal translation of the Persian originals FitzGerald worked with so imaginatively.

Of the 158 quatrains in the Ouseley manuscript, eighty-two involve drinking wine. On one or two occasions it is arguably the wine of love or the wine of life, and sometimes it may be the wine of divine wisdom, but often it seems to be just plain wine, mixed only with wit.

Although wine has rent my veil
So long as I have a soul I will not be separated from wine;
I am in perplexity concerning vintners, for they—
What will they buy that is better than what they sell?

Heron-Allen called Omar "a transcendental agnostic and an ornamental pessimist, as we have seen."[8] As proof, he might have cited,

Since no one will guarantee thee a tomorrow,
Make thou happy now this love-sick heart of thine;
Drink wine in the moonlight, O Moon, for the moon
Shall seek us long and shall not find us.[9]

Or rather,

Gaze as I may on all sides
In the garden flows a stream from the river Kausar,
The desert becomes like heaven, thou mayst say hell has disappeared
Sit thou then in heaven with one heavenly-faced.[10]

The River Kausar in Persian myth is the headstream of the Muslim Paradise. If this is pessimism it is a limited and almost sunny sort. The author of these quatrains finds the simple life not just wise, but pleasant, and he is willing to be pleased. Instead of destroying or undercutting this life on earth, the poet gives it weight and importance precisely because it is short and uncertain.

The last four quatrains in the Ouseley manuscript treat themes that FitzGerald highlighted in his version. But here they are Omar's or, at least, Omarian work. One of them gives us the scene most often associated with the *Rubaiyat*:

> If a loaf of wheaten bread be forthcoming
> A gourd of wine, and a thigh-bone of mutton
> and then, if thou and I be sitting in the wilderness,—
> That would be a joy to which no sultan can set bounds.[11]

Besides simple joys and pleasures there is also a kind of Sophoclean or Yeatsian darkness in Omar, a bare-knuckled realism, an unillusioned acceptance of death as the end of it all. Yeats translated Sophocles, saying, "Never to be born is best, ancient writers say . . . Second best's a gay goodnight and quickly turn away." And the next to last quatrain in the Ouseley manuscript says bluntly:

> Had I charge of the matter I would not have come,
> And likewise could I control my going, where should I go?
> Were it not better than that, that in this world
> I had neither come, nor gone, nor lived?

But the final quatrain in the Ouseley manuscript is an ironic salute to the last day of Ramadan, when observing Muslims are released from their month-long observance of daytime fasting and abstention from wine. The quatrain and the manuscript end with what might be just allegorical wine, but it is also an invocation of everyday street life in the person of the wine porter with his load of bottles. The quatrain marks a turn from the voluntary deprivations of Ramadan to hope and even to joy.

The month of Ramazan passes and Shawwal comes,
The season of increase and joy and story tellers comes
Now comes the time when "bottles upon the shoulder!"
They say—for the porters come and are back to back.[12]

Chapter 10

LATER LIFE AND LAST DAY OF
OMAR KHAYYAM

AFTER 1095, WITH Nizam and Malik-Shah dead, with both the Sunni caliph of Baghdad and the Shi'ite caliph of Cairo dead and without clear successors, with a fifteen-year-old Sultan Barkiyaruk, son of Malik-Shah, presiding over a shrinking empire, and with people of Ghazali's quality in retreat from public life, the world in which Omar Khayyam lived and wrote was drastically changed and significantly fragmented. Hasan-i Sabbah was holed up in his mountaintop eagle's nest, Alamut, from which he dispatched his legion of political hit men who spread fear and panic throughout Persia. The list of Hasan's assassinations grew steadily through the early decades of the twelfth century, almost every assassination being followed by a frenzied retaliatory slaughter of whatever Ismaelis could be identified or rounded up. In 1112, for example, some two hundred of Hasan's followers were tracked down and killed one by one in Aleppo. After Nizam al-Mulk's death at the hands of these Assassins, viziers succeeded one another rapidly. One historian notes grimly that after Nizam "the number of viziers who escaped being murdered, imprisoned, or having their wealth confiscated was small."[1]

Malik-Shah was also gone, and the remaining Seljuqs quarreled and divided up the empire. Another of Malik-Shah's sons,
Sanjar, was at first sultan only of Khorasan; he later reunited the
Seljuq empire briefly (Omar Khayyam was an honored and
consulted adviser to Sultan Sanjar).

Outside Islam to begin with, but now encroaching on it,
the First Crusade ground its way toward Jerusalem, finally
seizing it on July 15, 1099. In the surrounding Seljuq lands,
children of dead sultans, princelings, momentary or opportu-
nistic kings, and semi-sultans quarreled and negotiated and
fought. Occasionally one or another of the Seljuq princes would
reach out to Khayyam, often for trivial reasons. Could he think
of something to scare the birds away from a crop? Would he
please predict the weather for a hunting party? A new Islamic
century, the year 500 A.H.—much feared in anticipation—
arrived on September 2, 1106. This same year Ghazali resumed
teaching, not at Baghdad, but more modestly at Nishapur.
Ghazali would die in 1111; Hasan-i Sabbah would die in 1124.
During the first quarter of the twelfth century, we have
only occasional glimpses of Khayyam. He survived Malik-
Shah; he survived Nizam al-Mulk; he survived Ghazali and
he even survived Hasan-i Sabbah. Whatever else he was, Omar
Khayyam was a survivor.

In 1159, a writer named Nizami Arudi Samarqandy, looking
back on events, wrote:

In the year 1109, in the quarter of the slave traders of Amir
Bu Sa'id, I saw Imam Omar Khayyam and Imam Muzaffar
Isfizari and I heard from Hujjat al-Haq [an honorific title

meaning "the evidence of truth"] Omar that he said, "My grave will be in a location that every spring the north wind will spread flowers upon my grave."

These are rash words in Islam, for, as the Qur'an says; "No man knows where he shall die."

Omar's own last day came on December 4, 1131, and was recorded by his son-in-law, Imam Muhammad Baghdadi. Khayyam was then eighty-three. He had outlasted most of his friends and associates; and he was still studying, now Avicenna's *Shifa*, a comprehensive account of the whole of ancient knowledge, both theoretical and practical. It has four parts, logic (which includes rhetoric and poetics), physics (including psychology, plants, and animals), mathematics (including condensed versions of Euclid's elements and an outline of Ptolemy's *Almagest*), and metaphysics. There have been suggestions that the philosopher-mathematician Khayyam and the poet Khayyam were two different persons. There have also been suggestions that Omar was not a religious person in the ordinary sense of those words. But the account of his last day, recorded by his own son-in-law, suggests instead that there was indeed one person who was at least an outwardly conforming Muslim, certainly a dedicated philosopher, and also a man who, even at the end, had the wit of a poet.

He was studying the Shifa [recorded his son-in-law], while he was using a golden toothpick, until he reached the section on . . . "unity and multiplicity." He marked the section with his toothpick, closed the book and asked his companions to gather round . . . When his companions gathered, they stood up and prayed and Khayyam refused to eat or drink until he performed his night prayer. He prostrated [himself] by putting his forehead on the ground and said, "O Lord, I know you as much as it is possible for me; forgive me, for my knowledge of you is my way of reaching you" and then died.[2]

So perhaps there was only one Omar Khayyam after all. Disparate and competing abilities often exist side by side in the same person. How often the scholar with the subtlest grasp of the subject also has the most developed sense of fun; how often the person who really hungers for religious truth turns to irreverence when belief falters, and how often that irreverence is directed against an authority that promises but doesn't deliver.

Edward FitzGerald, writing seven hundred years later, would have understood Omar's deathbed remark.

Oh Thou, who Man of baser Earth didst make
And ev'n with Paradise devise the snake:
For all the Sin wherewith the Face of Man
Is blacken'd—Man's forgiveness give—and take!

And Robert Frost would have understood, too. One of Frost's late poems goes, in its short-winded, far-sighted entirety:

Forgive, O Lord, my little jokes on thee,
And I'll forgive thy great big one on me.

Interlude

THE DESTRUCTION OF NISHAPUR

THE WORLD OF Omar Khayyam is gone today, separated from us not only by nine centuries, but also by a long series of almost incomprehensible disasters both natural and man-made. The city of Nishapur has been destroyed—obliterated—over and over by massive earthquakes, and its population was exterminated in the thirteenth century by the Mongol invaders. Visiting Persia in 1889, Lord Curzon, the Governor-General of British India, said of Nishapur that it had been destroyed and rebuilt more times than any other city in history.[1] Situated in an area of frequent earthquakes, Nishapur was rebuilt after each quake, but the destruction was often so complete that a whole new site was selected for the rebuilding. Present-day Nishapur, a modest city of some 240,000 people, occupies the fourth known site for the city; it is some three miles northwest of its previous location, which is now only a vast field of ruins, "where only mounds, the footings and lower parts of mud brick walls and barely recognizable weathered stumps of buildings remain."[2]

The earthquakes destroyed everything but the people of Nishapur; the Mongols took care of the people. When Hulagu

Khan, grandson of Genghis Khan, set out in the thirteenth century to crush the Ismaili Assassins, who were by that time operating from some fifty castles or strongholds throughout Persia, he and his army of mounted warriors essentially wrecked ancient Persia, and virtually exterminated its urban populations in a campaign of coordinated destruction that was far more deadly than the never-ending earthquakes. The Mongols perpetrated a systematic ordered-from-above mass extermination of the entire civilian population of city after city. The Nishapur massacre of 1221 was just one of a number of unremembered holocausts of appalling proportions.

The Mongol invasion of Persia in the thirteenth century is one of the great catastrophes of history. Edward G. Browne, the influential historian of Persian literature, describes the invasion: "In its suddenness, its devastating destruction, its appalling

Nishapur

ferocity, its passionless and purposeless cruelty, its irresistible though short-lived violence, this outburst of savage nomads, hitherto hardly known by name even to their neighbors, resembles rather some brute cataclysm of the blind forces of nature rather than a phenomenon of human history."[3]

The Mongols sacked Baghdad in 1258, killing some 750,000 men, women, and children. Palaces, mosques, libraries—all were destroyed. The Tigris River ran black with ink from the thousands of books dumped into it. The caliph, symbolic head of Islam, was captured, rolled up in a rug, and ridden over by Mongol horsemen. (It was how they treated their own disgraced rulers; one did not distress the earth with the blood of rulers.) Damascus surrendered and its people survived. Aleppo did not, and when the Mongols took the city they butchered its fifty thousand inhabitants. The city of Harem, two days' march from Aleppo in the direction of Antioch, offered to surrender to Hulagu if he would treat the inhabitants fairly. He so swore, then massacred the entire population of the city for having offended him by doubting his word.

At Nishapur, which fell to the Mongols in the first wave of the onslaught in 1221, less than a hundred years after the death of Omar Khayyam, a Nishapurian Muslim border guard happened one day to kill the husband of Taghachar, the daughter of Genghis Khan. She retaliated by ordering the deaths of everyone in the city. The figure has been estimated as high as 1.7 million persons. "The heads of the slain were cut off, lest any living creature might be overlooked amongst them, and built into pyramids, the heads of men, women and children being kept apart."[4]

The Mongols were horsemen. They had no capital cities; the seat of the government was the saddle on the leader's horse. Their armies needed no lines of communication or supply. They moved with flocks of animals, the flesh of which was their only food. Requiring nothing but some grassland, they destroyed everything else. Despising farmers and city dwellers alike, they tore up the aqueducts, ruined the crops, plundered the cities, and pulled down the walled Persian gardens, the *para daezas* that gave us our word *paradise*. "The prime fact of Mesopotamian history," says Robert Byron in *The Road to Oxiana*, "is that in the thirteenth century Hulagu destroyed the irrigation system; and from that day to this Mesopotamia has remained a land of mud deprived of mud's only possible advantage, vegetable fertility."[5]

The devastation and depopulation of Persia by the Mongol invasion persisted for centuries, creating a cultural gulf between old Persia and modern times. Old Persia was essentially gone after the thirteenth century, making it difficult if not impossible for us to get a full sense of the great culture—the Golden Age of Islam (essentially the eighth to the eleventh centuries)—that lies on the far side of the split, the gulf created by the invasion.

And beside the physical destruction and the wholesale slaughter, a third thing separates us from Omar Khayyam's world: a nine-century-wide abyss of lightly regarded history. Eleventh-century Persia is utterly unfamiliar to most of us. We may have some idea of the Battle of Hastings in 1066 or the taking of Jerusalem in the First Crusade in 1099, but who has even heard the names of Nizam al-Mulk, Alp Arslan, or

Malik-Shah? Medieval Persian history is largely a blank for most of us, who would be hard put to name any figure between Darius I (550–486 B.C.E.) and Timur, also called Tamerlane (1336–1405 C.E.). Most of us cannot read the Persian language; few even know what it is called. The Arabic script in which modern Persian—Farsi—is written does not read left to right, but right to left. We are at best foggy about Persian geography. Is Nishapur east or west of Baghdad? North or south of Isfahan or Shiraz? Closer to Kandahar or Samarcand?

The modern writer on medieval Persia still risks the rebuke delivered in the middle of the eighteenth century by Samuel Johnson to Richard Knolles, author of *The Turkish History*. Knolles, said Johnson, wasted his efforts "upon a foreign and uninteresting subject, recounting enterprizes and revolutions of which none desire to be informed."[6]

Eleventh-century Persia had emerged from Zoroastrianism to become an Islamic culture, and, indeed, the center of Islamic culture. Modern Western thought can barely identify such major figures as Avicenna, al-Ghazali, and Averroes, and those generally only through their western names. Apart from Marco Polo, who traveled through Persia in 1273, and the *Arabian Nights*, which center on the eighth-century Baghdad of Haroun al-Rashid, we know little of these centuries and that little is mostly myth and legend.

Omar Khayyam's world lies on the far side of this great gulf and it still calls to our world despite the many and formidable obstacles that block our understanding of his world and his work. Western interest in Persian poetry is of long standing. German, French, English, and American writers have turned to the great Persians, and if we do not always remember Firdawsi, or Jami, or Sadi, we know a little about Hafiz, Rumi, and Omar Khayyam. Persian poetry is a cultural silk road. Through it we can trace the connections between Omar's world and ours. Intellectual and religious history are parts of the journey, which winds through Victorian England and Edward FitzGerald, but the main thread is the poems themselves, which bridge more successfully than anything else the vast gap between that time and this. The world of Omar Khayyam is dead and gone but his poetry has lived on.

> *Iram indeed is gone with all his Rose,*
> *And Jamshyd's Sev'n-ringed Cup where no one knows;*
> *But still a Ruby kindles in the Vine,*
> *And many a Garden by the Water blows.*

Part II

RUBÁIYÁT

OF

OMAR KHAYYÁM,

THE ASTRONOMER-POET OF PERSIA.

𝔗ranslated into 𝔈nglish 𝔙erse.

LONDON:

BERNARD QUARITCH,

CASTLE STREET, LEICESTER SQUARE.

1859.

Cover of first edition of FitzGerald's *Rubaiyat*, 1859

Chapter 11

LONDON, 1861: FITZGERALD'S
RUBAIYAT APPEARS

O NE DAY IN early July 1861, a thirty-year-old Celtic scholar named Whitley Stokes stopped in front of Bernard Quaritch's publishing house in Castle Street in London, and looked through the books and pamphlets on offer in the penny box. He picked out a thin thirty-four page pamphlet that called itself *The Rubaiyat of Omar Khayyam*. The title page said "Translated into English Verse," but the translator's name was not given. It had been published in 1859 and had not sold well; it was effectively being remaindered. We may suppose Stokes read the first couple of quatrains:

> *Awake! For Morning in the Bowl of Night*
> *Has flung the Stone that puts the Stars to Flight:*
> *And Lo! The Hunter of the East has caught*
> *The Sultan's Turret in a Noose of Light.*

> *Dreaming when Dawn's Left Hand was in the Sky*
> *I heard a Voice within the Tavern cry,*
> *"Awake, my Little ones, and fill the Cup*
> *Before Life's Liquor in its Cup be dry."*

Stokes bought two or three copies. Perhaps a little later, he bought up the remaining copies in the box. He was an Irish philologist, and, later, an Anglo-Indian jurist. He was a contributor to the *Saturday Review*. He was also friends with some of the writers in London, and he gave a copy of his new find to Dante Gabriel Rossetti, who was then thirty-three. He also gave a copy to the Irish poet Samuel Ferguson.

Rosetti showed the *Rubaiyat* to Algernon Swinburne, who was twenty-four at the time, and soon the poem was known to George Meredith, age thirty-three, to William Morris, age twenty-seven, to Edward Burne-Jones, then twenty-eight, and to John Ruskin, then forty-two. None of them knew who the translator was. The *Rubaiyat* was thus quickly launched (though it was two years after publication) and—importantly— admired on its merits, and not, as literary sociology so easily shows in so many cases, on the previous reputation of the author.

When a second edition, significantly revised and expanded, appeared in 1868 with the translator's name still withheld, and the title page reading "Rendered into English verse," an influential American writer and editor, Charles Eliot Norton, happened to be in England. Edward Burne-Jones's wife, Georgie, lent Norton her copy and Norton soon wrote a long enthusiastic review, which he published in the *North American Review* in October 1869.[1] The *Rubaiyat* Norton reviewed, the second edition, began:

Wake! For the Sun beyond yon Eastern height
Has chased the Session of the Stars from Night

And, to the field of Heav'n ascending, strikes
The Sultan's Turret with a Shaft of Light.

Norton's review not only praised the *Rubaiyat*, it also included seventy-seven complete quatrains (there were 110 in the second edition). Norton's review was thus effectively the first American edition of the book, and brought the *Rubaiyat* to wide attention. Norton was also the first to praise the English poetry of FitzGerald's translation as a major poetic achievement, parallel to but independent of the poetic achievement of the original Persian, a judgment that would be repeated many times. Of the still anonymous translator Norton wrote, "He is to be called 'translator' only in default of a better word, one which should express the poetic transfusion of a poetic spirit from one language to another, and the re-presentation of the ideas and images of the original in a form not altogether diverse from their own, but perfectly adapted to the new condition of time, place, custom and habit of mind in which they re appear." Norton knew something about translation; this same review was in the first place a review of a French edition of 464 quatrains of Khayyam's translated into French prose. "In the whole range of our literature," the review continues, referring to FitzGerald's English, "there is hardly to be found a more admirable example of the most skillful poetic rendering of remote foreign poetry than this work of an anonymous author affords. It has all the merit of a remarkable original production, and its excellence is the highest testimony that could be given to the essential impressiveness and worth of the Persian poet. It is the work of a poet inspired by the work of a poet, not a copy, but a reproduction, not a translation, but the re-delivery of a poetic inspiration."[2]

The unknown poet-translator was a bohemian scholar-gypsy masquerading as a Victorian gentleman; his name was Edward FitzGerald. Who was he really, and how had he come to produce his extraordinary book of verses?

Chapter 12

FITZGERALD'S FAMILY
AND EARLY YEARS

E DWARD FITZGERALD WAS born Edward Purcell at
Bredfield in Suffolk on March 31, 1809. His father, John
Purcell, was the son of a wealthy Dublin physician. John Purcell
married his first cousin, Mary Frances FitzGerald, took her
family name, fathered eight children, then sunk his entire
fortune into a Manchester coal mine owned by his wife.
Defeated by unstoppable flooding in the mine and cheated
by people he worked with, John Purcell died a bankrupt. A
weak, colorless man, Purcell was completely overshadowed by
his splendid wife, Mary Frances, who had a large independent
fortune and was said to be the wealthiest commoner in England.
The FitzGeralds were an ancient Anglo-Norman family "that
had been in Ireland for more than six centuries, during which
they had built up their position through reckless warfare and
prudent marriages until they were one of the three great families in control of the country."[1] Mary Frances was a very grand
lady and, we are told, a Junoesque beauty. Surviving portraits
show the haughty commanding quality if not the beauty.

Edward was the seventh of her eight uniformly neglected

children. The nursery, which she seldom visited, was in a gable on the top floor of her large Jacobean home called Bredfield House near the village of Woodbridge in Suffolk. Her son remarked that he and his brothers and sisters were "not much comforted" by their mother's infrequent visits to the nursery. "Descended from the fiery earls of Kildare," wrote one of FitzGerald's biographers, "she inherited their temperament and bore herself like a queen."[2] She traveled around England in great state with "an army of flunkeys and ladies maids," and was rumored to have sat for more than twenty portraits and studies by the great society painter Sir Thomas Lawrence. Mary Frances FitzGerald had at least six homes, each an estate; she dashed from one to another in a bright yellow coach pulled by four perfectly matched black horses. Her children were so intimidated by her that they would hide in the bushes in front of Bredfield House to watch her arrivals and departures. When she inherited a property called Little Island, a three-hundred-acre estate on an island in the Woodbridge River, she had herself "rowed in state across the river with twenty-four musicians playing in the barge." She ran her home on principles set out and described in the eighteenth-century novel *Clarissa*.[3] She gave great formal dinners, confronting her guests with gold-plated tableware and lavish place settings. She had her own box at the Haymarket Theatre and would sometimes summon one of her children to accompany her. She wore black velvet and diamonds; her many houses had brocaded walls and gilded satin furniture, deep rugs, stables for the horses, and kennels for the dogs. Edward remembered in later life how he had watched from the nursery window as his father and one

Squire Jenny "in scarlet hunting habits, whips in hand . . . rode across the lawns, surrounded by their pack of restless harriers."[4]

Edward FitzGerald grew up surrounded by bourgeois, genteel, conventionalizing forces, surrounded too by people who thought that high living meant conforming to the social norms of high society. Nothing in FitzGerald's childhood gives the slightest hint of the person he was to become; nothing links him to Persia or Persian poetry. Nothing links him to anything but Mr. Pickwick's England, with one exception. When he was seven years old FitzGerald spent time with a curious local figure, who took an interest in the boy, taking him for walks and talking to him about faraway places. His name was Edward Moor. A retired army major who had seen service in India, he wore a huge white hat, many sizes too big, which rested comically on his ears, and he always carried the same oddly elaborate walking stick made from the wood of an old English battleship, the *Royal George*. Major Moor had become interested in Hindu religion, had published a volume called *The Hindoo Pantheon*, and had amassed a large collection of Indian bronzes and paintings at his house in Great Bealings, a small village just a few miles from Bredfield House and the FitzGeralds. The strange artwork and the trophies—Major Moor installed an obelisk on his grounds—must have at least suggested to the young FitzGerald that another world besides that of Victorian England was out there somewhere.

Major Moor aside, the chief interest today in FitzGerald's wealthy, privileged, ostentatious upbringing is its complete absence in FitzGerald's poetry. The *Rubaiyat* turns its back on Victorian social life, on noble houses, stately dinner parties, elaborate and lovingly traced ancestry. Great business or social enterprises do not exist in the *Rubaiyat*. Later in life, in full revolt against his class, his family, and their values, FitzGerald would not even introduce his friends to his family. In his masterpiece, the *Rubaiyat of Omar Khayyam,* neither family nor Family plays any part at all. The *Rubaiyat* gives us a world emptied of ancestors and descendants, empty too of fathers, mothers, and children.

Chapter 13

SCHOOL YEARS

HOME AND FAMILY provided young Edward with a privileged, comfortable, but emotionally cold world; by great good fortune, however, he was sent off to a nearby boarding school where he flourished, making friends he would keep all his life. Starting in 1818 when he was nine, FitzGerald spent most of the next eight years of his life at the King Edward VI Grammar School in Bury St. Edmunds. It was not a large school; there were fewer than 160 students. The headmaster, Dr. Benjamin Heath Malkin, was anything but the typical English schoolmaster. He was warmly remembered by his students as "broad-minded, kindly and humorous," while his wife was equally well-remembered as a lively and caring mother figure to the boys.[1] Malkin was a friend of William Blake. When tragedy struck the Malkins in 1802—their six-year-old son Thomas, a prodigy who could read and write when he was three, died suddenly—Benjamin wrote *A Father's Memoirs of His Child*, for which Blake designed the frontispiece. This book was the first published account of Blake, who figures in the volume, which also contains the first regular printing of Blake's poem "The Tyger." It is the book through which Wordsworth and Coleridge first knew of Blake. Malkin's great loss was young Edward's gain, for Malkin ran a benevolent school, lavishing attention and affection on young boys who must have reminded him every day of his own loss. Dr. Malkin forbade fagging and bullying at the school. He took boys to the theater or had them over for dinner. The curriculum included good manners, the Catechism, English grammar, literature, and "the best Greek and Latin classics." The school was unusual for its emphases on literature and on essay writing. It would have been impossible for young FitzGerald not to have heard about Blake during these years, and indeed FitzGerald was well aware of Blake in 1833 when he was twenty-four and Blake, who had died in 1827, was still largely unknown.[2]

Three things about FitzGerald's time at the Edward VI School stand out. First, the fatherly influence of Malkin and the motherly influence of his wife made the school more homelike than FitzGerald's actual home. Second, the Malkins' connection with Blake, because it was a part of daily life, and connected with personal tragedy, was more real than "literary." What we think of as literary life—that is, an exotic or specialized, hard-to-reach lifestyle—was, for FitzGerald and his friends, just part of ordinary life. William Blake's poetry and engravings were not exotic museum pieces, but part of the daily heartbreak of a much-loved headmaster. The third outstanding thing about the school was the friendships it made possible and the resulting loyalty shown by its students.

FitzGerald was an inconsistent student: He was ranked first of twenty-one students his first year, thirteenth of twenty-one his second year, and fourth of fourteen his last year. But he was happy at school, and in later years he returned frequently to his old school haunts, just as he kept up with a number of his old school friends.

One of these friends was James Spedding, a prosperous farmer's son who was teased for his very high forehead. He was called Jem at school, where he had many friends. A quiet boy, and an excellent student, he was interested in Shakespeare, and FitzGerald once said, "I never heard him read a page but he threw new light upon it." Spedding's home was in the Lake District of England, and he knew William Wordsworth well enough to be his host when the poet visited Trinity College. Spedding would later spend (or *waste*, as FitzGerald thought) forty years producing a monumental edition of the works of Francis Bacon. FitzGerald was close enough to Spedding to complain candidly that while Spedding's new edition of Bacon was intended to clear Bacon's character, Bacon's works did not need re-editing and his character "could not be cleared." Spedding could hand it out as well as take it. He once said FitzGerald's literary judgments were "strange and wayward." FitzGerald and Spedding remained close friends as long as they lived.[3]

Another of FitzGerald's new friends at Bury St. Edmunds was William Bodham Donne, who was descended from the great English poet on his father's side and from the eighteenth-century English poet William Cowper on his mother's. FitzGerald's friendship with Donne, like his headmaster's friendship with Blake, was another of the circumstances that made literature a common aspect of daily life for FitzGerald and his friends, something taken more or less for granted. Donne was a gentle,

genial boy who later became librarian of the London Library
and a prolific writer on many subjects. He was offered the
editorship of the *Edinburgh Review*, but he turned it down. A
popular boy, a college friend once said of him, "Many men are
liked, but Donne is *loved*." Donne liked the Edward VI School so
much he later moved to Bury St. Edmunds to put his own children in his old school. FitzGerald visited Donne frequently
there and once wrote to another friend, "I shall spend my time
here wholly with my dear Donne, who shares with Spedding
my oldest and deepest love."[4] When FitzGerald's *Rubaiyyat of
Omar Khayyam* was finally published in 1859, FitzGerald sent
out only three copies of the anonymous pamphlet; one of the
three went to Donne.

A third school friend, John Mitchell Kemble, was the son
of the great English actor Charles Kemble and brother of the
actress and author Fanny Kemble. FitzGerald vividly remembered "Jacky" Kemble declaiming Hotspur's speeches from
Henry IV, Part One and John Dryden's ode "Alexander's Feast."
Kemble had trouble deciding on a career, eventually becoming
a well-known scholar of the Anglo-Saxon language.

John's sister Fanny too would be a lifelong friend and
correspondent of FitzGerald's. The twenty-year-old Fanny
Kemble's portrayal of Juliet in a production of Shakespeare's
Romeo and Juliet at Covent Garden Theatre in London in 1830
caused a sensation. One perceptive member of the audience
wrote, "She seemed too good for Romeo—her execution of
the last scene was as original as simple and sublime—no tossing
about and dragging her convulsions. She came forward on one
knee, drove the dagger into her heart with the calmest look of

desperation—she gave a look of deep agony, turned her head round with a smile of triumphant defiance, bounded up as with a tremendous convulsion and fell flat on her back—the impression was quite awful."[5] Fanny Kemble was not only a strikingly beautiful woman as Thomas Sully's two portraits show, she was also spirited, and "always ran or hiked ahead of the group, rode the fastest horse and climbed to the highest point."[6] Fanny Kemble later went to America, married a man named Pierce Butler who had vast land holdings and hundreds of slaves in the Georgia Sea Islands, quarreled with him (over slavery), divorced him, and became a prolific author.[7] She and FitzGerald carried on a lifelong and lively correspondence. It was Fanny's daughter, Sarah Wister, mother of the novelist Owen Wister, who first guessed, from far-off Philadelphia, in 1870, by reading Charles Eliot Norton's review of the second edition, who the anonymous "translator" of the Rubaiyat really was.

—

FitzGerald left school at seventeen, in 1826, and entered Trinity College Cambridge. It was not a great physical distance from the Edward VI School to college—Cambridgeshire is the next county west of Sussex—but Trinity was socially and intellectually a whole new world, one that FitzGerald came quickly to embrace wholeheartedly.

The young FitzGerald had a soft round face with highly arched eyebrows and a perpetually startled appearance. His nose was long and straight, and he had an unusually fleshy, vulnerable-looking mouth and a deeply cleft chin. His bright blue eyes flashed incongruously—and occasionally imperiously—from a dark face. He weighed almost two hundred pounds and was almost six feet tall.[8] The only photographs we have of FitzGerald were taken late in his life and they show a large sagging man, serious, sorrowful, rumpled, and penitentially sober. But we also have a much livelier though lesser known image of the young FitzGerald, a pencil drawing by one of his good friends that shows FitzGerald as a college student attending a math cram session yet gazing wistfully past the math problem at who knows what. It is much easier to imagine this person bringing out the *Rubaiyat* than the ancient, weary wreck of the photographs. In the drawing we can see the origin of such lines as these, from quatrain 27:

Myself when young did eagerly frequent
Doctor and Saint, and heard great argument
About it and about: but evermore
Came out by the same door where in I went.

Many of his friends from the Edward VI School went with FitzGerald to Cambridge. Kemble had entered Trinity the year before; Donne went the same year as FitzGerald, though to a different college; Spedding entered Trinity the following year. Kemble, Donne, and Spedding all went for the honors degree but FitzGerald worked toward an ordinary degree, a so-called pass degree (as did Charles Darwin and the historian Thomas Macaulay), because the path to an honors degree at Cambridge lay through the unsurmountable thicket of higher mathematics. Trinity was, after all, Newton's college, and nobody was ever allowed to forget it.

The curriculum had three parts. Natural philosophy (mostly mathematics), theology and moral philosophy (mostly proofs of Christianity, such as William Paley's *Evidences*), and Greek and Latin literature. The key piece of any Cambridge education was the tutor. Each student met his tutor once a week. FitzGerald's tutor was a historian named Connop Thirlwall who later translated Schleiermacher and wrote an immense *History of Greece*. FitzGerald later recalled how Thirlwall "took a little fancy to me, I think."[9] The master of Trinity at the time was Christopher Wordsworth, youngest brother of the poet.

FitzGerald loved college life from the start. He took rooms outside the college with a Mrs. Perry at 19 Kings Parade; his living room on the second floor was reached by a steep set of stairs, almost a ladder. Both the living room and the bedroom on the next floor up above looked out on Kings College Chapel. FitzGerald threw himself into college social life, where a breakfast party in a student's apartment might include "eggs, ham, beefsteaks, fowls, tongues, pies of all kinds, champagne, porter, ale, coffee, chocolate, tobacco and snuff." An evening wine party might offer "wines white and red, fruits, apples, grapes, oranges, French plums, almonds, and raisins, filberts, preserves, a sponge cake and cherry brandy."[10] College life included paying visits on acquaintances, or walking or rowing to nearby Chesterton—which was off-limits—to play bowls or billiards and drink ale. There were many meals to be taken together. FitzGerald had a marked interest in music, played the piano, and made four-part arrangements for singing. He joined the Cambridge musical society called Camus.

Spedding, Donne, Kemble, and a young poet named Alfred

Tennyson all belonged to the Cambridge Conversazione Society, which had only been founded six years earlier, in 1820. Membership was limited to twelve and so the group was generally known as the Apostles. Their goal was "to make men study and think on all matters except mathematics and classics professionally considered."[11] Even though he was not a member, FitzGerald was closer to the Apostles than to any other college group, and he shared their social and intellectual space. The Apostles were a lively and close-knit group. Each member tried to see each of the others at least once every day. The Apostles made a cult of friendship, setting "good company and platonic friendship above intellectuality as an apostolic attribute."[12]

The life FitzGerald discovered at Trinity and among the Apostles effectively set his social compass and intellectual style for the rest of his life. He remained, quite deliberately, a perpetual student, always on the move, always free to take up a new subject or a new friend. FitzGerald's later life was, as far as he could make it so, just an extension of college life and Apostolic comradeship, though without the muffling weight of an institution or the exclusionary rigidity of a club limited to a dozen members.

During his last year at Trinity, FitzGerald met and was immediately drawn to a young man named William Thackeray, with whom he quickly discovered he had a great deal in common, and soon after graduation became friends with Alfred Tennyson. Looking back at his time both at Edward VI and at Trinity College, what stands out is a realization that literature was in the daily air he breathed, not just in the books he studied. Poets and writers, Wordsworth, Donne, Cowper, Kemble, and Tennyson were not dim, unknown, or distant, but friends, relatives of friends, unavoidable parts of everyday life. FitzGerald would never play the part of a literary insider, a member of the literary establishment, but it is plain that from an early age he believed that what people did was write and that the lives they were leading would turn into literature as they went along.

The other thing that stands out about FitzGerald's time at Trinity, as at Edward VI, is the emphasis on friendship and the lifelong friends he made there. It was friendship too of a certain kind, intense, warm, demanding, pervasive, and of overriding importance. One of the most deeply appealing things about the *Rubaiyat* is the way it emphasizes, implicitly to be sure, intimacy—whether between friends or lovers—as the highest good in life, easily superior to wealth, fame, career, position, or accomplishment, and yet within reach of anyone.

And if the Wine you drink, the Lip you press,
End in what All begins and ends in—Yes;
*   Think then you are TO-DAY what YESTERDAY*
You were—TO-MORROW you shall not be less.

Chapter 14

THACKERAY

WILLIAM THACKERAY WAS eighteen, FitzGerald twenty when they met in 1829 in the rooms of Thackeray's tutor. FitzGerald was hoping to learn enough mathematics from the tutor to pass his exams. A friendship with Thackeray sprang up immediately. The two were very different but they hit it off with ease. FitzGerald called his new friend Will, Willy, or Thack, while Thackeray called Edward Ned, Neddibus, Neddikins, and Yedward.

Born in Calcutta to English parents who were both from families of Indian civil servants, the young Thackeray was a great bear of a man, six feet three inches tall with a broad full face. He was handsome, with strong features and a great shock of wavy hair. An only child, he was sent off to England for schooling at an early age. He hated school, but he loved to eat and drink; he rode horseback and liked spicy peppers. He cared little for academic routine, lasting only a year and a half at Trinity, but he was full of fun and skilled at drawing and caricature. FitzGerald would later remember Thack singing as he climbed the stairs to a friend's rooms. His drawing of a young

FitzGerald gazing abstractedly into space above a closed math book is the most vivid and appealing portrait we have of FitzGerald (see page 92).

Thackeray left Cambridge with no degree and no regrets. While at Trinity, he lost fifteen hundred pounds ($150,000 in today's money) to professional gamblers, and when, at age twenty-one, he inherited twenty thousand pounds (roughly two million dollars in today's money), he burned through it in just over a year, buying a magazine, *The National Standard*, that failed in thirteen months, investing in two Indian banks, both of which failed, and continuing to lose at gambling.

Thackeray had a taste for society and the life of balls and dinners, a taste that FitzGerald lacked, but he was also the only one of FitzGerald's friends who came to know his mother well. Thackeray was a frequent guest at Mrs. FitzGerald's dinners and he was the recipient of expensive and sometimes embarrassing gifts from her. Once she gave him a waistcoat made of tabinet, a damask-like fabric of wool and silk, a garment "so fine with its emerald and gold that I blushed," he said, "to wear it." Mrs. FitzGerald was, said Thackeray, "stupendously gracious" to him and in fact she was a perfect representative of the English high life that Thackeray so admiringly pilloried in his wildly successful novel *Vanity Fair*, which came out in 1847–48.[1]

When FitzGerald graduated from Trinity in February 1830, the first thing he did was go to Paris, where he seems to have dawdled about until early April when Thackeray suddenly showed up and Paris became attractive and absorbing. The two of them eagerly took in the sights and walked the boulevards,

Sketch of the young FitzGerald at Trinity by
William M. Thackeray

eating, smoking, and drinking too much. Staggering through the streets at night, Edward would stop to sing along with the organ grinders and their barrel organs. After three weeks Thackeray disappeared as suddenly as he had arrived. With him gone, Paris lost its attraction for FitzGerald and by mid-May 1830 he had gone back to Cambridge and to his old rooms with Mrs. Perry.

Thackeray and FitzGerald kept up a strong friendship over the years, carried on, like many of FitzGerald's friendships, mainly by correspondence. In the summer of 1831, for example, just a little more than a year after their time in Paris, the two friends fell into what FitzGerald later called a "red-hot correspondence" and an "immortal summer of foolscap."[2] Each of them started a letter to the other one every Sunday, keeping the letter at hand and adding to it daily until Sunday came around again and the letters—with handwriting covering "nearly every square inch of four foolscap pages"—would be closed, sealed up, and sent off, and a new one started. The two friends used the letters almost the way one uses the telephone or manages a blog. In the one surviving letter from this series, FitzGerald talks about his religious doubts, about the theater, about Shakespeare, Byron, Hume, Helvetius, and Diderot; there are two original poems, one of six stanzas, the other of four. FitzGerald talks about walking, about singing, about Irish history, but especially, perhaps, about friendship.

"So think of meeting me not as I am in my letters (for they being written when in a good humour, and read when you have nothing better to do, make all seem alert and agreeable) but as you used to see me in London, Cambridge, etc. If you

William M. Thackeray, portrait by Samuel Lawrence

come to think, you will see there is a great difference. Do not think I speak thus in a very light-hearted way about the tenacity of our friendship but with a very serious heart, anxious lest we should disappoint each other, and so lessen our love a little. I hate this subject and to the devil with it."[3] FitzGerald is one of the great letter writers in English. There is ease and intensity, immediacy and perspective, a willingness to live in the present, and an unconcealed yearning. This same letter concludes, "I see few people I care about, and so, oh Willy, be constant to me." This need for friendship, for closeness, lay right on the surface. FitzGerald once wrote another friend, John Allen, "I am an idle fellow, of a very lady-like turn of sentiment: and my friendships are more like loves, I think."[4]

The friendship with Thackeray lasted. In 1852 when Thackeray set out for America and put his affairs in order he wrote FitzGerald, "I mustn't go away without shaking your hand, and saying Farewell and God Bless you . . . I should like my daughters to remember that you are the best and oldest friend their Father ever had." Thackeray died in 1863, only fifty-two. Frederick Tennyson said he looked old, white, massive, and melancholy. Asked by his daughter Anne "which, of all your friends, have you cared for most," Thackeray said, "There was 'Old Fitz,' and I was very fond of Brookfield [another old friend from Cambridge days] once." He paused, then added, "We shall be very good friends again in hell together."[5]

We can see the shadow of Thackeray in the *Rubaiyat*. He is the friend who by repeated demonstration of personal feelings rises above the dreadful social level, and his is the spirit of satirical or ironic distancing from family and from the social and political present. The puppet master of *Vanity Fair* would have approved, for example, FitzGerald's quatrain:

> *We are no other than a moving row*
> *Of Magic Shadow-shapes that come and go*
>   *Round with the Sun-illumined Lantern held*
> *In Midnight by the Master of the Show.*[6]

Chapter 15

TENNYSON

IN 1870, THE sixty-one-year-old FitzGerald commissioned Samuel Lawrence to paint a portrait of a sailor friend, "Posh" Fletcher, "to hang up by old Thackeray and Tennyson, all three having a stamp of Grandeur about them in their several ways, and occupying great places in my Soul."[1] Alfred Tennyson was the best poet FitzGerald was to know well.

Six feet tall and powerfully built, when he was young he threw a heavy iron bar over a haystack in Somersby, Lincolnshire, where he was born and raised. Two locals, standing by, said no one else in the two parishes could have done it. Alfred was the fourth of twelve children. He was exactly the same age as FitzGerald, who was the seventh of eight. Five of Alfred's brothers and three sisters also wrote poetry. Thomas Carlyle, the leonine Victorian prose writer and public scrapper, the Mencken of his day, deep friend of Emerson's, author of unsparing books about heroism, Oliver Cromwell, the French Revolution, and Frederick the Great, left a vivid physical description of Tennyson. "One of the finest-looking men in the world. A great shock of rough, dusky, dark hair; bright, laughing hazel eyes; massive aquiline face, most massive, yet most delicate: of sallow brown complexion almost Indian looking, clothes cynically loose, free and easy, smokes infinite tobacco. His voice is musical, metallic, fit for loud laughter and piercing wail, and all that may lie between."[2]

Tennyson entered Trinity in 1828; his father would not let him leave home until he could recite from memory all the odes

Painting of the young Alfred Tennyson by Samuel Lawrence

of Horace. It took days. At Trinity Tennyson became a member of the Apostles and was casually known by FitzGerald during his last two years at college. The young poet was bohemian, utterly indifferent to convention; he ate, drank, and smoked too much. One friend watched him eat dinner in a tavern one night—two chops, one pickle, two cheeses, one pint of stout, one pot of ale, and he smoked three cigars. One friend guessed he smoked his pipe nine hours a day, another thought it was more like twelve. He would take up a sheet of manuscript and—carefully respecting the text—tear off the unwritten-on margin, rolling and twisting the blank paper into a spill to light his pipe.

FitzGerald and Tennyson became good friends after college, probably in 1835, but FitzGerald remembered the young Tennyson reciting such old English and Scottish ballads as "Clerke Saunders" and "Helen of Kirkconnel."

Oh, would I were where Helen lies
For night and day on me she cries
Oh, would I were where Helen lies
On fair Kirkconnel lea.

Tennyson also read aloud from Wordsworth, Keats, and Milton, and he read his own poems too, from a little red book into which he had copied them. He was a very effective reader-aloud, "mouthing out his hollow 'o's and 'a's, his voice very deep and deepchested," FitzGerald recalled, "but rather murmuring than mouthing, like the sound of a far sea or of a pine wood."[3]

FitzGerald and Tennyson visited Spedding at his home in Ambleside in 1835. Out rowing one day on Windermere, Tennyson recited a couple of lines from his manuscript poem "Morte d'Arthur":

Nine years she wrought it, sitting in the deeps
Upon the hidden bases of the hills.

"Not bad, that, Fitz, is it?" Tennyson asked. During the same trip FitzGerald just happened to start a sentence with "A Mr. Wilkinson, a clergyman . . ." "Why, Fitz," said Tennyson, "that's a verse, and a very bad one too." This set up a sort of game in which each tried to find the weakest line of iambic pentameter in the language. The scene is memorable for its ebullience, the playful, high-spirited, and almost always literary fun FitzGerald enjoyed with his friends. Tennyson was a voluble and spirited participant. Years later, FitzGerald remembered how Tennyson used to act out the "gunpowder-like" line in *Paradise Lost*, "So started up in his foul shape the Fiend." Tennyson would act out the line "with grim humour, from the crouching of the Toad to the Explosion." Tennyson also, in his earlier days, FitzGerald remembered, used "to do the Sun coming out from a cloud, and returning into one again, with a gradual opening and shutting of eyes and Lips etc. And—with a great fluffing up of his hair into full wig, and elevation of Cravat and Collar, George the Fourth in as comical and wonderful a way."[4] In a letter to another friend FitzGerald wrote, when he was twenty-nine, "We have had Alfred Tennyson here; very droll and very wayward; and much sitting up of nights til two or three in the morning with pipes in our mouths; at which good hour we would get Alfred to give us some of his magic music, which he does between growling and smoking; and so to bed."[5] A bit later he wrote, "A. Tennyson and I pass some hours together every day and night: with pipes and brandy and water. I hope he will publish ere long. He is a great fellow. But he is ruining himself by mismanagement and neglect of all kinds. He must smoke twelve hours out of the twenty-four."

FitzGerald was a deep admirer of Tennyson's early poems. He once wrote—and it may mirror his own slipping into greater and greater enjoyment of better and better poetry—"a man might forsake a drunken party to read Byron's 'Corsair': and Byron's 'Corsair' for Shelley's 'Alastor,' " and the 'Alastor' for the 'Dream of Fair Women' or 'The Palace of Art' [both by Alfred Tennyson]: and then I won't say that he would forsake these two last for anything of Wordsworth's, but his mind would be sufficiently refined and spiritualized to admit Wordsworth, and profit by him, and he might keep all the former imaginations as so many pictures or pieces of music in his mind."[6] Tennyson himself went into a ten-year hiatus when his 1833 volume, containing both the above-mentioned poems, was savagely attacked in the *Quarterly Review*. FitzGerald had reservations about some of Tennyson's later poems, but his admiration for the early ones never faded, and it was to Tennyson that FitzGerald wrote first when he began to read Omar Khayyam. Giving an account of a visit in 1856 to see his Persian teacher, Edward Cowell, FitzGerald wrote Tennyson, "We read some curious Infidel and Epicurean Tetrastichs by a Persian of the eleventh century—as savage against Destiny etc.

as Manfred—but mostly of Epicurean Pathos of this kind—
Drink—for the Moon will often come round to look for us in
this Garden and find us not."[7]

Tennyson's influence on FitzGerald's *Rubaiyat* is both general
and particular. Tennyson was the poet FitzGerald knew best,
Tennyson was the greatest Victorian master of poetic meter and
music, a skilled technician of sound. His poetry is "saturated with
regret, weariness, and death longing," but it is all expressed so
satisfyingly that it is not depressing but ennobling, even inspiring.[8]
Take these lines from "Tears, Idle Tears" for example.

> *Dear as remembered kisses after death,*
> *And sweet as those by hopeless fancy feigned*
> *On lips that are for others; deep as love,*
> *Deep as first love, and wild with all regret;*
> *O Death in Life, the days that are no more!*

What survives is first love and wildness, not hopelessness
or loss. FitzGerald became a master at the direct expression of
intimate feelings, as Tennyson was, and there is always a musical
and felicitous control of language that keeps FitzGerald's verse,
like Tennyson's, from bleakness and despair. Something close
to the Tennysonian music is all through FitzGerald, for example
in this quatrain:

> *Indeed, indeed, Repentence oft before*
> *I swore—but was I sober when I swore?*
> *   And then and then came Spring, and Rose-in-hand*
> *My threadbare Penitence apieces tore.*[9]

If FitzGerald paid close attention to Tennyson's work, Tennyson returned the compliment, even complaining once that FitzGerald had "borrowed" a line from "The Gardener's Daughter." The line in question was FitzGerald's "Starts for the dawn of nothing—O make haste." But Tennyson was working from memory. When he actually looked again at FitzGerald's line, he found it different enough from his own line—"The summer pilot of an empty heart/Unto the shores of nothing"— that he apologized to FitzGerald for having brought it up at all.[10] FitzGerald's masterpiece, like Tennyson's best poetry, works by a technical mastery largely veiled by perfectly achieved music. And Tennyson was finally very generous to his friend, writing in 1883 of "your golden Eastern lay,/Than which I know no version done/In English more divinely well;/A planet equal to the sun/Which cast it, that large infidel/Your Omar."[11]

Chapter 16

CARLYLE

FITZGERALD'S MOST INTERESTING and least likely friendship was with Thomas Carlyle. Born in 1795, the tough-minded, hard-bitten, enthusiastic Scot was already well known for his history of the French Revolution and for his book *On Heroes, Hero-Worship, and the Heroic in History* (1841), when he and FitzGerald met in 1842. FitzGerald later recalled Carlyle was "very handsome then, with his black hair, fine eyes, and a sort of crucified expression."[1] Carlyle was then forty-seven, FitzGerald thirty-three. FitzGerald knew of Carlyle before they met, of course, and had made arch comments in his letters about "an Englishman [who] writes of French Revolutions in a German style."[2]

In 1842 Carlyle was working on an edition of Oliver Cromwell's letters and speeches and had become interested in the Battle of Naseby (June 14, 1645), the pivotal battle of the Puritan revolution that defeated the English monarch Charles I. FitzGerald was in London in September 1842 and wrote his Quaker poet friend Bernard Barton: "I went to see Carlyle last night. He had just returned from the neighborhood of Bury.

He is full of Cromwell, and funnily enough, went over from
Rugby to Naseby this spring with poor Dr. Arnold. They
saw nothing, and walked over what was not the field of battle.*
I want him to go down with me, but he thinks it would be too
expensive. So I have engaged to collect what matter I can for
him on the spot."[3]

FitzGerald rushed to Naseby on his errand. A few days later
he reported again to Barton: "I have just seen some of the bones
of a dragoon and his horse [which] were found foundered in a
morass in the field—poor dragoon, much dismembered by
time: his less worthy members having been left in the owner's
summer house for the last twenty years have disappeared one by
one: but his skull is kept safe in the hall: not a bad skull neither:
and in it some teeth yet holding, and *bit of the iron heel of his boot*,
put into the skull by way of convenience . . . I have got a fellow
to dig at one of the great general graves in the field: and he tells
me tonight he has come to bones." FitzGerald was caught up
imaginatively. "Think of that warm 14th of June," he went on
to Barton, "when the Battle was fought, and they fell pell mell:
and then the country people came and buried them so shallow
that the stench was terrible, and the putrid matter oozed over
the ground for several yards: so that the cattle were observed to
eat those places very close for some years after."[4] It is sobering
to learn how much real life experience underlies some of the
well-known bits of the *Rubaiyat*. There is a good bit of Naseby
battlefield, for example, behind

---

* FitzGerald had at one time lived in a house on one of his family estates,
Naseby Wooleys, situated on the Naseby battlefield.

I sometimes think that never blows so red
The Rose as where some buried Caesar bled.

Carlyle was grateful to FitzGerald for his help with the Battle of Naseby, which he used in his book on Cromwell, and though they were of very different temperaments, Carlyle and FitzGerald became good friends. Some eight years after they met, FitzGerald could say of Carlyle "there is a bottom of truth in Carlyle's wildest rhapsodies."[5] As an example he might have noted that much as Carlyle admired Cromwell and could see the truth in Puritanism, he could also say, of English Puritan theology, "books equal in dullness were at no epoch of the world penned by unassisted man."[6] As Tennyson was for FitzGerald the great poet, and Thackeray was the great satirist, so Carlyle was the great moralist. FitzGerald found it easy and congenial to think of his friends in Carlylean terms of greatness. He would also have agreed with the Carlyle who said, "on the whole we make too much of faults; the details of the business hide the real center of it."[7] And Carlyle's central standpoint, that of a baffled, outraged, abandoned—but stubborn—believer, of sorts, is all through FitzGerald's work. Here is Carlyle's splendid and admiring description of the prophet Muhammed's basic situation: "What am I; what is this unfathomable Thing I live in, which men name Universe? What is Life; what is Death? What am I to believe? What am I to do? The grim rocks of Mount Hara, of Mount Sinai, the stern sandy solitudes answered not. The great Heaven rolling overhead with its blue-glancing stars, answered not. There was no answer. The man's own soul, and what of God's inspiration dwelt there, had to answer!"[8] And here is

FitzGerald, smoking with Carlylean outrage, even if it is neatened and shortened a bit.

What! out of senseless Nothing to provoke
A conscious Something to resent the yoke
   Of unpermitted Pleasure, under pain
Of Everlasting Penalties, if broke![9]

What! from his helpless Creature be repaid
Pure Gold for what he lent him dross-allayed—
   Sue for a debt he never did contract,
And cannot answer—Oh the sorry trade!

Thomas Carlyle

Perhaps the single most delightful image of himself FitzGerald left behind in his voluminous correspondence is his merry description of how, one evening three years after the battlefield excavation, he took his leave of Carlyle at the latter's home in London. Again to his friend Barton, FitzGerald wrote, "I spent one evening with Carlyle, but was very dull somehow, and delighted to get out into the street. An organ was playing a polka even so late in the street: and Carlyle was rather amazed to see me polka down the pavement—He shut his street door—to which he always accompanies you—with a kind of groan."[10]

Chapter 17

BACHELOR LIFE

DURING HIS TWENTIES and early thirties, FitzGerald led a footloose existence, though he had a home of sorts. He moved into Boulge Cottage, on a family estate, in 1837 and stayed there fifteen years. He traveled a lot, mostly in Suffolk and Norfolk. His moods varied from domestic contentment to social exuberance to personal loneliness. Many of his letters from this period have a cheerful and appealing quality, exuding at first glance a bright Pickwickian mediocrity. "Here I live with tolerable content," he wrote a friend from his sister's home, Geldestone Hall, near Beccles, in Norfolk, "perhaps with as much as most people arrive at, and what if one were properly grateful one would perhaps call perfect happiness. Here is a glorious sunshiny day: all the morning I read about Nero in Tacitus lying at full length on a bench in the garden: a nightingale singing, and some red anemones eying the sun manfully not far off. A funny mixture all this: Nero and the delicacy of Spring: all very human however. Then at half past one lunch on Cambridge cream cheese, then a ride over hill and dale, then spudding up some weeds from the grass: and then coming in,

I sit down to write to you, my sister winding red worsted from the back of a chair, and the most delightful girl in the world chattering incessantly. So runs the world away . . . Such as life is, I believe I have got hold of a good end of it."[1]

He was a very good, devoted letter writer; almost every letter has something about his reading, often at some length. But the main thing is that he just wrote. He asked one friend who had little free time to write him anyway, even if "ever so shortly" and "what-ever-aboutly." When he had nothing to write about, he wrote about that. "I have sat over this little sheet," he once wrote Barton, "a quarter of an hour, looking up and asking intelligence of the ceiling, the furniture of the room, and the lawn before the window; but no thought reducible to paper comes."[2]

A woman who had visited Boulge Cottage as a girl kept a lively remembrance of FitzGerald's place. "The chaos of the room is vividly in my mind. Large pictures standing against the walls. Portrait on an easel, books, boots, sticks, music scattered about on tables, chairs and floor. An open piano with music, lumber everywhere, so that there was a difficulty in emptying a chair for my mother to sit on." Sometimes FitzGerald would have a small party; Barton described one as having "lots of palaver, smoking, and laughing. Edward was in one of his drollest cues, and did the honours of his cottage with such gravity of humours that we roared again. It was the oddest mélange. Tea, porter, ale, wine, brandy, cigars, cold lamb, salad, cucumbers, bread and cheese . . . It was one continuous spread, something coming on fresh every ten minutes til we wondered whence they came and whither they could be put. 'Gentlemen, the resources of the cottage are exhaustless,' shouted our host."[3] Early FitzGerald biographers give us a glimpse of another party, in 1842, when Thackeray, Tennyson, Dickens, and FitzGerald went driving one afternoon, all in the same carriage, then had dinner at Dickens's home, after which they played cards and drank mulled claret. It sounds too perfect to be possible. FitzGerald found Dickens "unaffected and hospitable," adding, archly, that he saw nothing to suggest genius in Dickens's face except "a certain acute cut of the upper eyelid."[4]

If FitzGerald could be jolly and social, he was also lonely a good deal of the time, and he said so frequently. But we should be grateful for this, as one of his best biographers has pointed out. "It is not totally unfeeling to be thankful that he was lonely so much of his life, for out of that seclusion came his finest legacy to English Literature, the long series of thousands of letters by which he kept in touch with the world. Friendship, gaiety, love of literary and visual art in nearly every form, music, sensitivity to the changing seasons of Suffolk, the hard work of writing and translation, loving gossip about his acquaintances: all these inform his wonderful correspondence, in which only occasionally is the surface clouded by a shadow of the melancholy and loneliness that were such a basic part of his life."[5] FitzGerald's *Rubaiyat* too has some of those same shadows:

> *Come, fill the Cup, and in the fire of Spring*
> *Your Winter-garment of Repentance fling:*
> *The Bird of Time has but a little way*
> *To flutter—and the Bird is on the Wing.*

FitzGerald loved flowers, paintings, music, and above all books, and his letters, while giving off a large general feeling of satisfaction, often crackle with off-beat imaginative bits of observation. He noted how the flower vendors, men with baskets of flowers for sale, would cry out on the street, "Growing, Growing, Growing, all the Glory going!" Or he might advise a correspondent, "Pray get a small frame, concaving inwardly . . . which leads the eye into the picture, whereas a frame convexing outwardly leads the eye away from the picture."[6] Hardly a letter goes by without at least some talk of reading. He read everything, was interested in art, music, architecture, local history, gossip, the weather, the seasons.

FitzGerald loved spirited foolery. He and a small group of friends celebrated the coronation of Queen Victoria in 1838 by diving into a pond when they heard the distant cannon announcing the moment, swimming about and singing "God Save the Queen." Once, later in his life, he went to see the great English actor Sir Henry Irving play Hamlet. He thought it the worst Hamlet he had ever seen. When Irving got to the line, "something too much of this," FitzGerald called out from the pit where he was standing, "a great deal too much!" as he left to go back to his inn.[7]

Chapter 18

A FRIENDSHIP LIKE A LOVE: WILLIAM KENWORTHY BROWNE

IN LATE AUGUST 1832, the twenty-three-year-old FitzGerald struck up a conversation on the steam packet from Bristol to Tenby with a sixteen-year-old boy named William Kenworthy Browne. The resulting friendship became, in the words of FitzGerald's first biographer, "the great central circumstance of FitzGerald's life."[1] In a letter written twenty-five years later, FitzGerald described the "lad—then just sixteen—whom I met on board the packet from Bristol and next morning at the boarding house—apt then to appear with a little chalk on the edge of his cheek from a touch of the Billiard Table Cue—and now a man of 40—Farmer, Magistrate, Militia Officer—Father of a Family—and of more use in a week than I in my long life."[2]

Browne—his father had added the e to the family name—was not university educated (a condition much in his favor in FitzGerald's view), but was dedicated to the active life of riding, hunting, fishing, and amusement. He married, had children, and served in the army and as a local magistrate. He was full of common sense, and "not averse to books and literature, when pleasantly interpreted."[3]

Browne was a handsome lad. He stood five foot seven. Thackeray (who was huge) called him "little Browne." He had a pink and white complexion and was very good-looking, as can be seen in the portrait sketch of him FitzGerald commissioned from Samuel Lawrence. Lawrence also painted the young and handsome Tennyson and the pleasant if imposing young

William Kenworthy Browne, from an unfinished
portrait by Samuel Lawrence

Thackeray. All three of these paintings were done for FitzGerald by Lawrence and together the three images give a touching— they are so young!—sense of FitzGerald's world of friends.

FitzGerald was strongly attracted to Browne from the first, and continued every year to spend as much time as possible in his company, loafing, sketching, fishing, traveling. It is possible that FitzGerald was unaware of the exact nature of the physical attraction; however it is plain enough even though most of the correspondence between them has disappeared. It is equally possible that FitzGerald recognized strong male bonding in general terms as a common enough occurrence among men of his time and place. FitzGerald had many close male friends— and more than a few female friends as well—during his life- time, and he recognized his friendships as having the intensity of loves. "What passions our friendships were," wrote Thackeray of his college years. And FitzGerald wrote to another friend in 1834, in a phrase worth repeating, "I am an idle fellow, of a very lady-like turn of sentiment, and my friendships are more like loves, I think."[4]

"You and Browne," he wrote another friend, six years after meeting Browne, "have certainly made me more happy than any men living." FitzGerald was quite unabashed to observe that he felt he had some feminine traits in his mostly masculine makeup. Beside the "lady-like turn of sentiment" noted above, FitzGerald also admitted to having what he called "a very young lady-like partiality to writing to those I love."[5]

Exactly what FitzGerald's relationship with Browne was like we can only guess. The correspondence has disappeared, but FitzGerald wrote about his affection and admiration for Browne to many other friends and his language is more than admiring and affectionate—smitten is closer. FitzGerald could always express himself in letters in a personal, intimate, disarming way without really revealing much at all. In 1839, when Browne was twenty-three and FitzGerald an elderly thirty, FitzGerald wrote to Barton about Browne. "He has shot at rooks and rabbits and trained horses and dogs; and I—have looked at him: and well I may while I can, for his like is not to be seen . . . Perhaps also he will not be long to be looked at: for there are signs of decay about him, and his very perfection of nature somehow forebodes a short continuance. Indeed there is something anomalous and perhaps insupportable in the appearance of one perfect character in a world of imperfection and inconsistency."[6]

In late January 1859, when FitzGerald was about to turn fifty and Browne, then forty-three, was returning from hunting one day, Browne rode over to speak to another rider who was punishing his horse. The other horse kicked out at Browne's mare, which reared, lost its footing, and fell heavily backward directly on Browne, crushing the whole middle part of his body. He was carried home, where, expected to die, he lingered on for two dreadful months. Browne had been married for fifteen years and some distance had naturally grown between him and FitzGerald. The latter was only told of Browne's condition a few days before he died. He rushed to the bedside. "I went," he wrote his old friend Donne, "and saw—no longer the gay Lad, nor the healthy man I had known: but a wreck of all that: a Face like Charles I (after decapitation almost) above the Clothes: the poor shattered body underneath lying as it had lain eight weeks—such a case as the doctor says he had never known. Instead of the light utterance of other days, too, came the slow, painful syllables in a far lower key: and when the old familiar Words 'Old Fellow—Fitz' etc came forth so spoken, I broke down too."[7]

Browne's death was "the most crushing blow of [FitzGerald's] life," and it came on the very day that saw the publication of his greatest achievement, the *Rubaiyat of Omar Khayyam*.[8]

The next day was FitzGerald's fiftieth birthday. Perhaps it occurred to him that he had already written an epitaph for Browne. The twenty-first quatrain of the *Rubaiyat* reads:

> *Lo! some we loved, the loveliest and best*
> *That Time and Fate of all their Vintage prest,*
> *   Have drunk their Cup a Round or two before,*
> *And one by one crept silently to Rest.*

Chapter 19

POETRY

THE *RUBAIYAT* PUBLISHED in 1859 had been long in the making. FitzGerald had loved poetry from an early age. His first published poem, "The Meadows in Spring," written when he was twenty-two, is an unremarkable lyric that might give hope to any young poet, since it is hard to believe that anyone capable of the *Rubaiyat's* excellence could be this mediocre in the beginning, the last line reaching for a sort of Tennysonian repetition.

> *'Tis a dull sight*
> *To see the year dying*
> *When winter winds*
> *Set the yellow wood sighing:*
> *Sighing, oh! sighing.*[1]

In spite of his gentlemanly diffidence and his chronic and lifelong modesty, FitzGerald had strong and often original responses to particular poems. At twenty-three he was rereading Shakespeare's sonnets, finding in them "the very essence of tenderness that is only to be found in the best parts of his Romeo and Juliet besides. I have been truly lapped in these sonnets for some time," he wrote to his friend John Allen, "they seem all stuck about my heart, like the ballads that used to be on the walls of London."[2] A year later he had discovered—or perhaps rediscovered—William Blake's work, and he wrote, again to Allen, "to me there is particular interest in this man's writing and drawing, from the strangeness of the constitution of his mind. He was a man that used to see visions: and make drawings and paintings of Alexander the Great, Caesar, etc who, he declared, stood before him while he drew."[3]

He came to Keats early too, some six years before Monckton Milnes's *Life, Letters and Literary Remains of John Keats* brought him to wide general notice. When the Milnes book did come out, FitzGerald wrote Frederick Tennyson, Alfred's brother, "By the by, beg, borrow, steal, or buy Keats' Letters and Poems; most wonderful bits of poems, written offhand at a sitting, most of them. I only wonder that they do not make a noise in the world."[4]

He kept up with both Tennysons, being particularly close to Frederick and sometimes a little wry about the much better known Alfred. Of the latter's "In Memoriam," he wrote his friend Donne, "Don't you think the world wants other notes than elegiac now?"[5] FitzGerald admired Wordsworth's poetry, but he could, upon occasion, speak tartly of the man himself. "There's that great metaphysical, Doric, moral, religious and psychological poet of the age, W. Wordsworth, who doesn't like to be contradicted at all, nor to be neglected in any way."[6] FitzGerald read Latin, Greek, Spanish, and, eventually, Persian, and was attentive to poetry in all those languages. He may have been interested in grand poetic effects; he was certainly attentive to poetic detail. He wrote Fanny Kemble one day about Robert Burns: "Do you know that one of Burns' few almost perfect stanzas was perfect till he added two syllables to each alternate line to fit it to the lovely Music which almost excuses such a dilution of the Verse?

> *Ye Banks and Braes o' bonnie Doon*
> *How can ye bloom (so fresh) so fair?*
> *Ye little Birds how can ye sing,*
> *And I so (weary) full of care!"*[7]

This reveals one of FitzGerald's greatest strengths as a poet. From his fond recollections of the poems declaimed at school to his playful banter with Tennyson to such details as this little note about Burns, FitzGerald could always depend on his ear, his attention to meter, to the poetic line, to the music of poetry.

Poets and indeed poetry itself were for FitzGerald an expected and habitual part of everyday life. Not surprisingly his *Rubaiyat* has been widely read, often by people who do not read a great deal of poetry. One key to FitzGerald's ability to reach so many is his own generous assumption that a great many, perhaps even most people, have it in them not just to read but actually to write poetry. "There are few men," wrote FitzGerald to Barton, "who have leisure to read, and are possessed of any music in their souls, who are not capable of versifying on some ten or twelve occasions during their natural lives."[8]

Perhaps it is also the common touch in FitzGerald that has led to the condescension with which he is so often received, though no one has been harder on him than he was on himself. He wrote one friend that he only possessed "what Goethe calls the 'Barber's talent' of easy narrative of easy things—can tell of Barton and Chesterton Inn but not of Atreus and the Alps."[9] He was not always so rough on himself. He could also write, while hard at work on the *Rubaiyat*, "I really think I have the faculty of making some things readable which others have hitherto left unreadable." But even that is too modest. The quatrain, whether Persian or English, is not generally considered one of the great poetic forms. But just as Wordsworth and Coleridge could make great poetry from ballad meter, and just as Emily Dickinson could do great things with hymn meter, so FitzGerald, at his best, could make great and lasting poetry out of the common quatrain or ruba'i.

Chapter 20

FITZGERALD AT WORK: EDITING AND ASSEMBLY; THE EXAMPLE OF BARTON

WHEN FITZGERALD'S FRIEND Bernard Barton the Quaker poet died, FitzGerald extracted from his nine published volumes of poetry enough passable work to make one small volume. FitzGerald's approach to Barton's work shines a spotlight on his own way of working and his method of composition.

FitzGerald prized Barton as a friend, and after his death worked with Barton's daughter, named Lucy, on the memorial volume, for which he wrote a brief personal account, published by Hall Virtue and Company of London in 1849 as *Memoir, Letters, and Poems of Bernard Barton*. Daughter Lucy was presumed by the public to be the editor, though it appears that FitzGerald did most of the work. He selected, revised, and rewrote the best things from Barton's volumes. His assessment of Barton's work is cool, and quite the opposite of overstatement. To an inquiry about Barton's work from Donne, FitzGerald replied, "Thanks for your letter. As far as I can see nothing of BB's would have a general interest except a Small Selection of his Poems; and a short Memoir, with a few letters, by way of specimens of the

Man. From what I have seen of his letters, I cannot imagine there is any more in them than ease and good humour: of which a little is enough for the world at large."

FitzGerald went on to describe how he handled Barton's poetry. "I have now looked over all his volumes with some care; and have selected what will fill about 200 pages of print—as I suppose—really all the best part out of 9 *volumes*! Some of the poems I take entire—some half—some only a few stanzas, and these dovetailed together—with a change of a word, or even of a line here and there, to give them logic and fluency." FitzGerald had given Barton's work a searching reading. "It is wonderful when you come to look close into most of these poems to see the elements of repetition, indistinctness etc. which go to make them diffuse and weary. I am sure I have distilled many pretty little poems out of long dull ones which the world has discarded."

FitzGerald was well aware that his editing practices were unconventional, even dubious. Still writing to Donne, he questioned: "As a matter of *Art*, I have no doubt whatsoever I am right: whether I am right in *morals* to use a dead man so I am not certain. Tell me candidly what you think of this."[1]

FitzGerald enjoyed a liberated attitude toward what we now call intellectual property. He found it reasonable to edit, revise, and rearrange whole books and even paintings as well as individual poems to meet his own standards. Once he bought a large painting of a fruit girl by John Opie. He cut it down, borrowed paint and brushes, and "lay upon the floor two hours patching over and renovating . . . It has now to be varnished," he wrote to a friend.[2]

Another time he cut a painting down the middle "making two very good pictures," he assured a correspondent.[3] He liked to fill in the dark corners of old paintings with gold, making an oval within the rectangular frame. FitzGerald handled books the same way he did paintings. He edited and rearranged and rebound many volumes of other people's work. "His library contained many volumes that he had revised to suit his taste. He cut down books to one half or one third of their original length, and bound them with others, which he had treated similarly." Acting on an impulse many a reader has entertained only in fantasy, FitzGerald literally chopped big books down to size. "Works of two or three volumes he reduced to one. Sometimes he wrote in a paragraph to supply the context of a deletion."[4] FitzGerald was a tinkerer, a reviser, an editor as much as an original writer. Once he made an abridgment of Samuel Richardson's million-word-long novel *Clarissa*. Another time he edited down for one of his nieces Dickens's *The Old Curiosity Shop* to just the narrative of little Nell's travels.

FitzGerald would treat the work of Omar Khayyam no differently. And given good material, he could produce spectacular results. Not much could be done with the good Barton's ordinariness, but the Persian material he would soon come to love offered a great deal of room for creative combination and judicious assembly. The memorable fifth quatrain of the *Rubaiyat* is a good example:

Iram indeed is gone with all his Rose,
And Jamshyd's Sev'n-ringed Cup where no man knows

But still a Ruby kindles in the Vine
And many a Garden by the Water blows.

No single Persian source for this quatrain has been found. Jamshyd, a ruby in the wine, and a garden by the water occur separately in quatrains attributed to Omar, but the Garden of Iram does not. FitzGerald took up a loose group of evocative images and made a hauntingly good and very Persian-sounding quatrain of his own. The emotions evoked, of nostalgia for a grand past and an opposite and saving openness to the simple present, are strong and memorable. FitzGerald has here given old material the power of originality.

Chapter 21

FITZGERALD AND PERSIA

IT IS POSSIBLE that FitzGerald first became aware of Persia when he was fifteen and heard his friend John Kemble declaim John Dryden's "Alexander's Feast" at school at Bury St. Edmunds; the poem begins, "'Twas at the royal feast, for Persia won." Or perhaps it was even an earlier and more general interest in the region that started when his neighbor, Major Moor, took the seven-year-old FitzGerald for walks and talks about the major's time in India and his interest in the Hindu pantheon. FitzGerald would also have known some or all of the recent English poetry that was set in the Middle East: Byron's "Destruction of Sennacherib" (1815), Shelley's "Ozymandias" (1818) and his "Revolt of Islam" (1818). Leigh Hunt's "Abou Ben Adhem" came out in 1838, and Matthew Arnold's "Sohrab and Rustum" in 1853. And Carlyle's lecture on Mohammed appeared in his book *On Heroes, Hero-Worship, and the Heroic in History* in 1841.

Whatever FitzGerald's interest in the larger Middle East, his active interest in Persia and Persian poetry in particular really began in 1845, when he was thirty-six and first met Edward

Cowell. Son of a corn merchant in Ipswich, Cowell was then just nineteen, self-educated, and with a bit of a name for himself already gained through publishing translations from the Persian—including some odes of Hafiz—in the *Monthly Register* and the *Asiatic Journal*. Cowell was a prodigy; at eighteen he knew Greek, Latin, Italian, German, Old Norse, and some Sanskrit. Cowell was a good-looking younger man, though FitzGerald seems to have been drawn to him more through common literary and intellectual passions than anything else. Their friendship warmed quickly and they became very close, reading each other's suggestions and ranging widely into classics and Eastern literature, and spending a great deal of time together.

Something else soon bound them further. Two years after meeting FitzGerald, Cowell, now twenty-one, announced that he was going to marry Elizabeth Charlesworth, a vicar's daughter with whom FitzGerald had been half in love for years. Family legend has it that when Cowell announced his intention, FitzGerald replied, "The deuce you are! Why, you have taken my Lady!"[1] The marriage did indeed take place and soon the three of them became inseparable, often spending weeks together at a time.

By 1852, FitzGerald was starting the study of the Persian language with Cowell; in 1853 he published the result of his earlier interest in Spanish in a volume called *Six Dramas of Calderon*, described on the title page as "Freely translated by Edward FitzGerald." In November 1853 FitzGerald translated "The Gardiner and the Nightingale" from Sadi's *Gulistan*. The next year, 1854, he was reading Jami's *Salaman and Absal*. By 1855 he had produced a translation of this openly Sufi romance, sending it to *Fraser's Magazine*, which rejected it. He then had it privately printed in April 1856. The same month Cowell sent him copies of some of the quatrains attributed to the Persian mathematician and philosopher Omar Khayyam, quatrains Cowell had found in the beautiful Ouseley manuscript in the Bodleian Library at Oxford.[2]

FitzGerald was excited by the quatrains, to which he quickly bent his attention. He spent the last part of June and the first two weeks in July 1856 in a sort of farewell visit with the Cowells. During this time, Cowell gave FitzGerald a complete copy of the Ouseley Manuscript 140, which contained 158 quatrains. The Cowells had been determined since February to go to India, for Cowell had then been appointed a professor of history in the Presidency College in Calcutta. FitzGerald had been opposed to Cowell's going to Oxford. Now he opposed the move to India, frantically offering the couple a stipend to stay in England where they could all be together. Elizabeth Cowell had wanted Cowell to study at Oxford, and he had duly gone and had taken a prestigious degree. Now, when she wanted Cowell to go to India, he went.

When the Cowells sailed for Calcutta on August 1, 1856, it was, wrote FitzGerald's early biographer, "as a parting of lovers." FitzGerald felt the loss of Cowell as a "catastrophe."[3] FitzGerald had thanked Cowell in the foreword to his *Salaman and Absal*—"What scholarship it has is yours, my Master in Persian, and so much besides . . . "—and Cowell had given FitzGerald a book in which he had written some lines of verse, including two that read, "My soul is sick, nor can it be / At rest, 'til it find rest in thee."

Three short months after the Cowells sailed for India, FitzGerald walked himself into a second catastrophe. On November 4, 1856, he married Lucy Barton, daughter of his deceased friend the Quaker poet Bernard Barton. Lucy and Fitz were spectacularly unsuited to each other. She was forty-eight, he was forty-seven; neither had ever married. They were not in love. They had completely antithetical ideas of what constitutes the good life. FitzGerald seems to have married her to carry out an unstated pledge to his friend, who had died seven years earlier. Lucy had given up her Quaker ways and yearned to belong to the Norfolk gentry. She could take no pleasure in a dinner unless she could dress for it. FitzGerald was in headlong revolt not only against dressing for dinner, but against his class, his parents, and everything they stood for. He wore shabby clothes topped with an old slouch hat to his wedding; he had been known to take his shoes off and walk barefoot on the high road, and if he drank too much at a neighbor's house, and got sleepy walking home, he might lie down in the grass by the roadside and sleep until three or four in the morning before proceeding on home. Gentlemen just didn't do such things.[4]

In June 1857, eight months after his marriage with Lucy, FitzGerald received in the mail from Cowell a copy of another Omar Khayyam manuscript. This one was in the Bengal Asiatic Society Library and it contained 510 quatrains.[5] FitzGerald, who had spent much of his time since the Cowells' departure working on the Khayyam quatrains, redoubled his efforts, taking images, lines, and even whole quatrains from the Calcutta manuscript to supplement the material he was selecting out of Oxford's Ouseley Manuscript 140. In August 1857, one year after the

Cowells had left England and just ten months after the wedding, FitzGerald and Lucy Barton agreed to separate. A year and a half after this separation, FitzGerald's *Rubaiyat of Omar Khayyam* was published, on the last day of March 1859—less than three years after FitzGerald first saw the Oxford manuscript and first learned about Omar.

The work of rendering Omar's Persian poetry into English is the outstanding achievement of FitzGerald's life, several orders of magnitude beyond all his other writing. So it is sobering to realize—paying attention to the dates—that the work was begun under the shadow of a great loss, the Cowells' departure for India; carried on under the roughest domestic stretch of FitzGerald's life; and published on the very day his friend Browne died after lingering for a painful two months. The miracle is how FitzGerald made a thing of lasting beauty out of the losses, confusions, darkness, and misery of this period. "He is a man of real power," Cowell wrote his mother, "one such as we seldom meet with in the world. There is something so very *solid* and *stately* about him, a kind of slumbering giant, or silent Vesuvius. It is only at times that the eruption comes, but when it comes, it overwhelms you."[6]

Chapter 22

RENDERING *RUBAIYAT*

FITZGERALD OFTEN READ lying down, but he always wrote standing up, and he owned a writing table with a flat top at just the right height for him. This alone suggests that his frequent self-description as an "idle fellow" is not the whole story. In April 1856, for example, when Cowell first gave him the copies of selected quatrains from the Ouseley manuscript, FitzGerald was already far from idle and indeed deep in his Persian studies. He had had his English translation of Jami's *Salaman and Absal* printed, and had thought enough of it to send copies to some of the most eminent oriental scholars in England. F. Max Müller, editor of the grand fifty-volume edition of English translations of the *Sacred Books of the East*, wrote, via Elizabeth Cowell, to thank FitzGerald, saying, handsomely, "a poet, Jami, has found a poet, worthy to be his translator."[1] Copies were also sent to the aging poet Walter Savage Landor and to the great orientalist H. H. Wilson. Sending copies to such well-known figures clearly suggests that FitzGerald harbored a real hope for recognition, even if the anonymity of the *Rubaiyat* has suggested otherwise.

By January 1857 FitzGerald was writing Cowell, then in India, that he "read very little except Persian since you went."[2] What he was working on mostly was a translation of *The Bird Parliament* by the great Persian poet Farid-al-Din Attar (which is what FitzGerald would publish next after the *Rubaiyat*), but he was not neglecting Omar Khayyam. Indeed, by April 1857 he was writing the French orientalist Garcin de Tassy to ask if there were any Khayyam manuscripts in French libraries. De Tassy replied to FitzGerald, and was helpful and positive enough that FitzGerald was soon wondering aloud, in a letter to Cowell, as to who should be leading the work on Omar, de Tassy, Cowell, or FitzGerald himself. Omar was quickly becoming FitzGerald's central preoccupation. In May 1857, he wrote a friend that he was working on a "poor little Persian Epicurean, who sings the old standing Religion of the world, 'let us make the best of today, who can answer for tomorrow?'"[3]

FitzGerald's 1857 letters to Cowell are filled with questions, quotations, comparisons, observations, and analysis of Omar's quatrains. Like his earlier letters to Thackeray, FitzGerald would start one, then put it aside, usually tucked into his Ouseley manuscript, take it out again and add to it, then put it away again. After days or sometimes weeks of additions, FitzGerald would close up the letter and mail it off to India. Almost every letter ends ruefully. "I often wonder if I shall ever see you both again!" It was not an unreasonable thing to wonder about. India was a long way off. The Cowells' initial trip to India had taken four months. Letters sometimes took as long as five months, and an English person who made a career in India could expect perhaps one trip home to England before retirement. FitzGerald put a good face on the matter by saying that the letters between him and Cowell were really not much different than their previous letters back and forth from Norfolk to Oxford.

One long letter to Cowell has an entry for June 29, 1857, that demonstrates in vivid detail how FitzGerald actually worked. He was wrestling with quatrain number 137 in the newly arrived Calcutta MS 1548. The long missive is more a professional memo than a friendly letter. FitzGerald's syntax is strained; all his antennae are out. While the letter is hard to follow, it offers a solid answer to the obvious question about FitzGerald—"What about his Persian?"—and makes clear the level—the day-by-day temperature—of FitzGerald's linguistic engagement with the Persian originals. The lines FitzGerald parsed out word by word and phrase by phrase would soon come together as the opening stanza of the first edition of FitzGerald's *Rubaiyat*:

> *Awake! For Morning in the Bowl of Night*
> *Has flung the Stone that puts the Stars to Flight:*
> *And Lo! The Hunter of the East has caught*
> *The Sultan's Turret in a Noose of Light.*

In the following letter literal translations from Edward Heron-Allen enable a modern reader to follow FitzGerald's line of thought more fully.

June 29 [1857] Quatrain 137 خورشیدکمندصبح برپام افکند [literally "The sun casts the noose of morning upon the roofs"] seems one worth understanding: which I do not wholly, not being wholly able to decipher; especially the second and fourth lines. But I write about it now because it reminds me of a passage in Salaman I have more than once intended to tell you about. "The sun has thrown the noose of morning over the house-top; the *rouge-faced* day" (?—what else can I make of کیخسرورور [literally "Kai Khosru of the day"]) "has thrown the Pebble into the Cup" as a sign of breaking up the Party, says Johnson* at the word مُهره [lit. "Bead"] though in this case it does not mean breaking up any party but that of Night, whose departure is a sign for the Drinkers to assemble. It would have been pretty if one could construe "The Sun throws Day—or Day throws the Sun—into the Cup of Heaven as a signal for Night's retreat." But however this be, you must remember how often we have read about the Stone in the Cup, etc. Now I have not Salaman with me, but I have often thought that in that passage where the Shah finds the two lovers in their Island, drinking the Cup of Sorrow and Tears "Unshattered by the stone of Separation" I believe I have rendered it; but, had I seen Johnson's مُهره first, I should have translated—"The Cup of Tears," etc., *In which Farewell had never yet been flung*—with a note to explain about "the Stone," etc. I am not sure whether the original Salaman does refer to this; but the Image is so pretty and so smacks of the Desert Life—the Pebble thrown into the Cup and all starting to Horse—that it is worth risking it. So do you—you in Calcutta! emend your Salaman to this effect, will you?—And

---

* This is a reference to the Persian-English Dictionary used by FitzGerald.

so to go on with Quatrain 137. "Drink for the Crier" -(Query, whether Cock or Muezzin?) "of the Morning Station arising sends forth a Voice -(Query, an Evil-omened Voice?) "about the flight of Time"—No, that's not it; but your Munshi [scribe] writes the line آوازه شربو رزایام انکند [lit. "Hurls into the days the cry of "Drink ye"]. What makes me think it may be something as to the loss of a Night of Life, is the last quatrain but three in the MS. which I happened to glance at the other day; درقت سپیده دم خروس سحری [lit. "at dawn the morning cock"].[4]

FitzGerald was clearly fully absorbed, attentively comparing texts with dictionary in hand, weighing one against another, looking up words, questioning readings—intense and responsible work, more intent on fidelity to the original than on any creativity or originality of his own.

A month later, FitzGerald had reached what Emerson called "the casting moment," the all-important moment in which the shape of a project first becomes clear to the writer. Writing to Cowell in the middle of July 1857, on the one-year anniversary of their last meeting in England, FitzGerald was full of enthusiasm for the Omar "whom I decidedly prefer to any Persian I have yet seen." By late July he was, he declared, "so well interested in him [Omar] I can't let him go yet." A few days later, on August 6, he had his "aha" moment. "I see," he wrote to Cowell, "how a very pretty Eclogue might be tessellated out of his scattered Quatrains." FitzGerald was well aware that Persian collections of tetrastichs, rubaiyats, did not tell a story. Each four line quatrain is a separate, stand-alone poem. What FitzGerald now saw was a way to link some of these separate quatrains into a coherent whole.

His idea was to tell the story of a single day in the life of the poet. He had had what would turn out to be his closing quatrain in mind for about a year. Indeed, the quatrain that would end his *Rubaiyat* was the fifth in the Ouseley manuscript, which he had quoted to Alfred Tennyson when he first sat down to read Omar Khayyam with the Cowells. More recently, he had sent the same quatrain, Ouseley 5, to his friend the novelist George Borrow without a translation to go with it. The Persian for this quatrain looks like this:

چـون عهـده نمی کند کسی فردا را
حـالی خوش کن تو این دل شیدا را
می نوش بدور ماهای ماه که ماه
بسیار بجوید دنیا بد ما را

A literal translation reads:

Since no one will guarantee thee a tomorrow
Make thou happy now this lovesick heart
Drink wine in the moonlight, O Moon, for the moon
Shall seek us long and shall not find us.[5]

His opening became Calcutta 134, the details of which he wrestled with in his letter to Cowell. What remained was to arrange—to tessellate or assemble—a number of quatrains and parts of quatrains to make a satisfying whole out of a group of separate and only individually satisfying rubaiyat.

By late August 1857, FitzGerald had completed his second detailed examination of the Calcutta manuscript. All through the fall of 1857 he worked on the quatrains, until, in December, he was moved to stake an explicit claim. For a while he had

wondered whether de Tassy or Cowell should be the one to
present Omar to the modern world. But he was the one who
was most interested and now he stepped forward and said
so. "In truth," he wrote Cowell, "I take old Omar rather more
as my property than yours: he and I are more akin, are we
not? You see all his Beauty, but you can't feel *with* him in
some respects as I do."[6] And in fact the stay-at-home, amateur,
and freethinking FitzGerald had made a surer, deeper connection with the Persian poet than had the all-too-English and
Christian professor.

Sometime in December 1857 or January 1858, FitzGerald
did send off thirty-five quatrains and an introduction to
Fraser's Magazine. *Fraser's* sat on the submission for nearly a year.
FitzGerald continued to be deeply interested in Omar, kept
working on the verses, and waited nervously for word from the
magazine. A letter he sent to the poet George Crabbe sometime
in the spring ends, "Yours (with a bad finger—from morosely
biting it) E.FG." By November 1858 he still hadn't heard from
Fraser's and he wrote Cowell that he now wanted to take the
manuscript back and add "some stanzas which I kept out for
fear of being too strong." He predicted that Cowell wouldn't
like the result, but couldn't help adding, "Yet it is most inge-
niously tessellated into a sort of Epicurean Eclogue in a Persian
Garden."[7]

In January 1859, FitzGerald did as he had said he would;
he took back the manuscript from *Fraser's*, added some forty
quatrains, prefaced the seventy-five poems with an introduction (which was mostly a reprint of an account of Omar
Khayyam that Cowell had written and published in the *Calcutta*

Review, and which was duly acknowledged by FitzGerald), and arranged to have 250 copies of the booklet privately printed. The small booklets with their brown paper covers were ready by mid-February 1859. FitzGerald kept forty copies to give away and turned the rest over to the publisher and bookseller Bernard Quaritch.

Chapter 23

TRANSLATED OR RENDERED?

FITZGERALD COULD NOT have foreseen the amazing—the stupefying—success his work would have. By 1900 twenty rival translations of Omar Khayyam had appeared in English. By 1929 there had been 586 English editions of FitzGerald's *Rubaiyat*. It has been translated into at least fifty-four languages, and most of the translations are from FitzGerald, not from the original Persian. There have been twenty different translations into German, eleven different translations into Urdu, and eight into Arabic. The *Rubaiyat* has been translated into most common European and Asian languages and into Gujarati, Orissa, Tamil, Hindi, Marathi, Kashmiri, Punjabi, and Sanskrit. More than forty artists have illustrated the work. A copy of FitzGerald's *Rubaiyat* with illustrations— "accompaniments"—by Elihu Vedder, a huge book nicknamed "The Great Omar" measuring fifteen inches wide and nearly two feet high with a cover made of fifteen hundred bits of worked leather, set with 1,050 precious and semiprecious stones, was shipped in a custom-made "waterproof" box on the maiden voyage of the *Titanic*.[1]

But FitzGerald would not have been completely surprised at the long-running controversy over the accuracy and suitability of his translations from the Persian, and he discussed the problem often enough to have left a solid sense of what he was after, and an equally clear sense that he did in fact achieve what he set out to do.

In September 1858, before he took back his manuscript from *Fraser's*, he wrote Cowell saying, "My Translation will interest you from its Form, also in many respects in its Detail: very unliteral it is. Many Quatrains are mashed together: and something lost, I [don't] doubt, of Omar's Simplicity, which is so much a Virtue in him."² Clearly he was not aiming at a literal translation, yet he used the word "translated" on the title page of his first edition: "Rubaiyat of/Omar Khayyam/The Astronomer-Poet of Persia/Translated into English Verse." And the final paragraph of the short introduction begins, "With regard to the present Translation . . ." The paragraph goes on to emphasize that the original Persian rubaiyat are "independent stanzas" and that "those here selected are strung into something of an Eclogue."³

In April 1859, with the book just published, FitzGerald wrote Cowell with an admirably clear explanation of what he was after. "I suppose very few People have ever taken such Pains in translation as I have: though certainly not to be literal. But, at all Cost, a Thing must live: with a transfusion of one's worse Life if one can't retain the original's better [life]. Better a live sparrow than a stuffed eagle."⁴

The nineteenth-century theologian Friedrich Schleiermacher proposed in 1813 that a useful way of approaching the problem of translation might be to stop asking whether it was literal or not and start asking whether it aimed to move the reader back and closer to the original, or, the reverse, whether it aimed to pull the original forward and closer to the modern reader.[5] FitzGerald clearly and explicitly took the latter view, as may be seen from the prefatory letter he once attached to his translation from the classical Greek of *The Downfall and Death of King Oedipus*. "I pretend to very little more than representing the old Greek in sufficiently readable English verse: and whatever I have omitted, added, or altered, has been done with a view to the English reader of today, without questioning what was fittest for Athenian theatre more than two thousand years ago."[6] Of his translations from the Spanish dramatist Pedro Calderón de la Barca, FitzGerald said that while "faithfully trying to retain what was fine and efficient," he nevertheless "sunk, reduced, altered, and replaced much that seemed not."[7]

To make his approach a bit clearer, FitzGerald altered the wording of the title page of the second and subsequent editions of the *Rubaiyat* to read "Rendered into English Verse," even as he kept the phrase "with regard to the present translation" in the opening sentence of the paragraph of the introduction that explains his formal innovations. This second edition, expanded to 110 quatrains, was the one reviewed so favorably in 1869 by Charles Eliot Norton. Norton's comments fit closely with Schleiermacher's second type of translation—the kind that brings the original closer to the reader. Referring to the still unnamed author of the *Rubaiyat*, Norton wrote: "He is to be called 'translator' only in default of a better word, one which should express the poetic transformation of a poetic spirit from one language to another and the re-presentation of the ideas and images of the original in a form not altogether diverse from their own, but perfectly adapted to the new condition of time, place, custom, and habit of mind in which they re-appear." It is also fair to say that so far none of the other translations of Omar Khayyam into English after FitzGerald have come up to this mark.

In 1872, as FitzGerald and his English publisher Bernard Quaritch were approaching a third edition of the *Rubaiyat* (which would be cut back to 101 quatrains), FitzGerald threw a little more light on the structure of the book. "I daresay," he wrote Quaritch, "Edition 1 is better in some respects than 2, but I think not altogether. Surely, several good things were added—perhaps too much of them which also gave Omar's thoughts room to turn in, as also the Day which the poem occupies. He begins with Dawn pretty sober and contemplative; then as he thinks and drinks, grows savage, blasphemous etc. and then again sobers down into melancholy at nightfall. All which wanted rather more expansion than the first edition gave. I daresay Edition 1 best pleased those who read it first: as first impressions are apt to be the strongest . . . As to the relative fidelity of the two versions, there is not a pin to choose—not in the opening stanzas you send."[8]

In 1878 as the time for a fourth edition—also of 101 quatrains—approached, FitzGerald wrote an American man of letters about translation. FitzGerald's immediate subject was his translations from Calderón, but his comments show how consistent his approach was as he went from project to project. "I am persuaded," he told James Russell Lowell, "that to keep

Life in the work (as Drama must) the translator (however inferior to his original) must recast that original into his own likeness. The less like his original, so much the worse: but still, the live Dog is better than the dead Lion."[9]

Fifteen years after FitzGerald's death in 1883 his old Persian teacher and close friend Edward Cowell wrote a letter in response to one from a younger scholar named Edward Heron-Allen, who had become intensely interested in the Persian originals behind FitzGerald's work. Heron-Allen had learned Persian in order to follow this interest, and in 1898 he published a literal translation of the whole of the Ouseley Manuscript 140 from which FitzGerald had drawn much of his material. Next Heron-Allen meant to correlate FitzGerald's quatrains with all possible Persian sources. He wrote to Cowell to ask about FitzGerald's working methods. "I am quite sure," Cowell wrote back, "that FitzGerald did not make a literal prose version first, he was too fond of getting the strong vivid impression of the original as a whole. He pondered this over and over afterwards, and altered it in his lonely walks, sometimes approaching nearer to the original, and often diverging further. He was always aiming at some strong and worthy equivalent: verbal accuracy he disregarded."[10]

Almost two years later, in 1899, Heron-Allen published a volume called *FitzGerald's Rubaiyat of Omar Khayyam with Their Original Persian Sources*. Basing his work on FitzGerald's fourth edition, Heron-Allen reached the conclusion that forty-nine of the quatrains are "faithful and beautiful paraphrases of single quatrains from the Ouseley ms. or the Calcutta ms. or both." Forty-four more quatrains are "traceable to more than one quatrain and may therefore be termed composite." Those two categories account for 93 of the 101 quatrains in FitzGerald's fourth edition. Two quatrains, numbers 46 and 98, Heron-Allen declared to be inspired by quatrains FitzGerald found in Nicolas's French text. Two others reflect "the whole spirit of the original poem." Two more, numbers 33 and 34 "are traceable exclusively to the influence of the *Mantik-ut-tair* [*The Bird Parliament* of Farid-al-Din Attar]." Two quatrains, numbers 2 and 3, were "primarily inspired by Omar [and] influenced by the Odes of Hafiz."[11] Heron-Allen's meticulous conclusions have never been seriously questioned.

There is, to be sure, a good deal of interest in the all but impossible question as to which, if any, of the thousands of quatrains attributed to Omar Khayyam were actually written by him. One modern scholar, a poet, translator, and professor of Persian, Dick Davis, writes "I rather doubt that the historical Khayyam wrote poems in Persian at all."[12] The Khayyam scholar Mehdi Aminrazavi thinks the search for the "historical Khayyam" is misguided and says, "Despite all the various methods and techniques developed by scholars, it is virtually impossible to distinguish the authentic poems from the inauthentic ones." Other modern Persian scholars such as Ali Furughi, Ali Dashti, and Sadiq Hedayat are not widely agreed on which quatrains or how many were actually written by the historical Khayyam, and some scholars have pointed out that there are as many as four different men of the same name to be found in old records.[13]

It is too much to say that FitzGerald "translated a poem that did not exist," though surely we can agree with Iran B. Hassani

Jewett that FitzGerald's *Rubaiyat* is "an English poem inspired by a Persian poet." The critic Edmund Gosse went too far when he said FitzGerald's translations "must never be compared with the originals, or treated as translations at all. They should be judged on their own merits as poems . . . of faultless delicacy of diction." The closest parallel to what FitzGerald did comes from Proust, who said of his own translations of John Ruskin, "I do not claim to know English, I claim to know Ruskin."[14] FitzGerald could in fact read Persian, and he translated other and longer Persian poems. What the modern Persian scholar Hamid Dabashi has said, not about what is *lost*, but what is *found* in translations of philosophy, applies equally to poetry: "Works of philosophy and their readers gain in translation not just because these authors begin to breathe in a new language, but because the text signals a world alien to its initial composition. Above all they gain because these authors and their texts have to face a new audience."[15] FitzGerald was right when in 1859 his first edition of the *Rubaiyat* had just appeared and he wrote to Cowell—as bears repeating—"at all Cost, a Thing must live."[16]

Chapter 24

GERONTION: THE LAST YEARS
OF EDWARD FITZGERALD

A FTER PUBLISHING THE *Rubaiyat* in 1859, FitzGerald tinkered with it for the rest of his life. After publication of the fourth edition in 1879, he left a marked-up copy of it in a small tin box for his literary executor to use in bringing out a fifth edition, which appeared in 1889, six years after his death. FitzGerald's scrupulous attention to detail is at odds with the self-protective modesty of the note his executor, W. A. Wright, found in the tin box. The note said, "I do not suppose it likely that any of my works should be reprinted after my death." He was, of course, quite wrong about that, but the offhand and dismissive remark could easily be applied to the details of his life after and apart from the *Rubaiyat*. FitzGerald is an excellent example of a truth articulated by Hasidism, that every thing and every person and every situation contains within it a small spark of the divine, a spark that may with sufficient attention be nursed into a flame. FitzGerald himself believed there was a possibility of poetry in anyone who read much and had a little music in his soul.

FitzGerald knew he was onto something during the frenzied

and eager months of his first engagement with Omar in 1857. He was a good enough judge of poetry to know he was doing something first rate in the *Rubaiyat* and only in the *Rubaiyat*.

———

In appearance Edward FitzGerald was, in the words of one of his earliest biographers, Arthur Benson, "a tall, dreamy-looking man, blue eyed, with large sensitive lips, and a melancholy expression; his face tanned with exposure to the sun; moving his head as he walked, with a remote, almost haughty air, as though he guarded his own secret: strong and active from much exercise, and irresolute in his movements, with straggling grey hair, and slovenly in dress, wearing an ancient, battered, black-banded, shiny-edged tall hat, round which he would in windy weather tie a handkerchief to keep it in its place."[1]

He traveled a good deal during the last two decades of his life, on the Continent and all over his part of England, and he spent many summers on a small schooner yacht that he called the *Scandal* because it was the fastest thing around. In 1864, the fifty-five-year-old FitzGerald was smitten by a twenty-six-year-old handsome sailor named Joseph Fletcher. FitzGerald had a herring boat built for Fletcher to fish with. FitzGerald nicknamed Fletcher "Posh," and had the boat named *Meum and Tuum*, names which, like *Scandal* and its dinghy called *Whisper*, signal that a lot more was going on than met the eye.

FitzGerald had many friends—he had always had a real gift, a flair for friendship—and a large, semi-distant family, especially nieces. He made and received many visits, looked at many pictures, listened to all the music he could, wrote many and superb letters, read many books, and excerpted, corrected, reduced, refined, edited, collected, and reassembled enough texts to leave an imposing body of work. He kept one notebook called "Paradise" for great bits, balancing it with another called "Half-hours with the Worst Authors." He had a notebook labeled "Museum Book" for things he ran into in the British Museum, another for accounts of debates in Parliament. He assembled at least ten scrapbooks. By the time of the third edition of the *Rubaiyat* in 1872, he had done translations from Greek and Spanish literature as well as Persian, and was working on a project to record the sea-slang of Lowestoft, the fishing town where he kept his schooner and the easternmost point in the British Isles. He made his abridgment of Samuel Richardson's *Clarissa* and he edited and condensed the poet George Crabbe's 1819 volume *Tales of the Hall*. During his last years he worked on a preface for an edition of Dryden's works, on a guide to the correspondence of Madame de Sévigné, and on a biography of Charles Lamb, none of which he finished.

Carlyle died in 1881; so did Spedding, FitzGerald's friend from boarding school. Thackeray had died young, almost twenty years before. In 1882, Donne died. Dante Gabriel Rossetti, Darwin, Emerson, and Longfellow all died that same year. The great literary years of the nineteenth century were closing down. Edward FitzGerald died in his sleep, during a visit to his friend Crabbe, on June 14, 1883.

One of his early biographers noted how "FitzGerald's position with regard to the poetry that was rising and swelling about him is that of a stranded boat on a lee shore. He could not bring himself into line with modern verse at all; he had none of the nineteenth century spirit."[2] What FitzGerald did have was a premonition of the twentieth century and of modernism. T. S. Eliot was born in 1888, five years after FitzGerald died. In 1902, when he was fourteen, Eliot discovered the *Rubaiyat*. "I can clearly recall the moment," he wrote, "when at the age of fourteen or so I happened to pick up a copy of FitzGerald's Omar which was lying about, and the almost overwhelming introduction to a new world of feeling, which the poem was the occasion of giving me. It was like a sudden conversion— the world appeared anew, painted with bright delicious and painful colors." Eliot immediately set to work on what he later disparaged as "a number of very gloomy and atheistical and despairing quatrains," which he would later suppress. He may have lost his youthful enthusiasm for FitzGerald's poetry, but he never entirely abandoned the connection. When he reached the advanced age of thirty-one, Eliot set to work on "Gerontion," his difficult but haunting poem about being old. "Gerontion" opens:

> *Here I am, an old man in a dry month,*
> *Being read to by a boy, waiting for rain.*

Eliot had been reading or rereading Arthur Benson's book on FitzGerald written for the English Men of Letters series, especially the part where Benson prints appealing excerpts from FitzGerald's late letters. In between passages, Benson says, in his own voice, "Here he sits, in a dry month, old and blind, being read to by a country boy, longing for rain."[3] But Benson was not making this up out of whole cloth, any more than FitzGerald had made up the poetry of Omar Khayyam. What was moving about in Benson's mind as he wrote this was a passage in a letter FitzGerald wrote to Samuel Lawrence in 1883. "Here I still live," FitzGerald had written, "reading and being read to part of my time, walking abroad three or four times a day, or night." Two days after writing this letter FitzGerald died in his sleep. So his late, if not positively last, words survived him—changed to be sure—to become the opening of a famous modern poem thirty-five years later. The sentence from the letter had been reworked, reworded, improved. FitzGerald would have approved.

Chapter 25

THE LUCRETIAN PARALLEL

FITZGERALD'S *RUBAIYAT* IS essentially Persian poetry and it opens a window onto medieval Persia. At the same time, it must be said, the dominant organizing principles of FitzGerald's work are from a different tradition, namely the Lucretian/Epicurean tradition, and that worldview is arguably the most important intellectual strain in his book. Indeed, if Lucretius' *De Rerum Natura* (*On the Nature of Things*) is "the least visible of the great poems," as Burton Feldman has put it, FitzGerald's *Rubaiyat* is surely the most visible descendant of that great occluded original.[1] FitzGerald was deeply, openly, visibly involved with Lucretius and with the Epicurean philosophy for which Lucretius is the main source. At thirty, FitzGerald could write of the "Epicurean ease" of his life; at thirty-five he complained/boasted that he did nothing but read the same old books—Lucretius among them—over and over. When, at age thirty-eight, he read the scientist Charles Lyell with great enthusiasm, it was a scientific, up-to-date, and fundamentally Lucretian viewpoint he was admiring. Lyell, like Lucretius, and like the Stoics, believed that for answers to questions about the way things are, we need to turn not to bibles and priests, not to rulers or families, not to society or history, but to nature.

FitzGerald even translated a bit of *De Rerum Natura* in 1848—a bit that has apparently not survived—and when, years later, he began to read Omar Khayyam with his friend Cowell, FitzGerald saw the Lucretian parallel at once, writing playfully to Frederick Tennyson about the "infidel Epicurean Tetrastichs" on which he and the Cowells were spending time. As he worked on translating the Persian quatrains in 1858, grouping them into a loose narrative, he was explicitly thinking of his work of assembly as making "a sort of Epicurean Eclogue."[2]

Lucretius (circa 99 B.C.E. to circa 55 B.C.E.) is almost as interesting for the passion and enthusiasm with which he pitched his ideas as he is for the ideas themselves. With commendable indifference to his own "originality," he was committed fully and solely to the ideas of Epicurus, the Athenian philosopher (341 to 270 B.C.E.) who died 171 years before Lucretius was born. For Lucretius, Epicurus was not just an interesting philosopher with a new slant on things, but a godlike figure, a missionary and a healer who had come to save the human race by liberating it from fear, specifically from fear of the gods, from fear of death, and from fear of life and punishments after death. In the words of one modern translator and enthusiastic fan, Lucretius regarded Epicurus as "the spiritual savior of mankind. Epicurus is leader, father and god: he revealed the secrets of the universe: he raised mankind to heaven by his victory over superstition: he lightened the darkness and stilled the storms of the spirit: he revealed the truth and the whole truth."[3]

The Epicureans also believed that teaching is by personal contact; knowledge and wisdom pass from teacher to student, one by one. Lucretius' passionate admiration of Epicurus, his self-abnegation, and his avid embrace of Epicurean ideas make both Lucretius and his philosophy alive and deeply appealing. Here is Stephen Greenblatt's brilliant and moving summary: "The stuff of the Universe, Lucretius proposed, is an infinite number of atoms moving randomly through space, like dust motes in a sunbeam, colliding, hooking together, forming complex structures, breaking apart again, in a ceaseless process of creation and destruction. There is no escape from this process. When you look up at the night sky and, feeling unaccountably moved, marvel at the numberless stars, you are not seeing the handiwork of the gods or a crystalline sphere detached from our transient world. You are seeing the same material world of which you are a part, and from whose elements you are made. There is no master plan, no divine architect, no intelligent design."[4] When Carl Sagan said "we are star-stuff" he was echoing Lucretius.

Lucretius is strong medicine. Gods exist, but they live in a world apart from ours and have nothing to do with us. Lucretius' cold-eyed conclusion is that we are not now and we have never been worth a moment's notice from them. There is nothing for them in us. Lucretius asks, sarcastically, "For what largess of beneficence could our gratitude bestow upon beings immortal and blessed, that they should attempt to effect anything for our sakes?"[5] Worshipping the gods is not only foolish, it is wrong and leads to evil. Before he is a hundred lines into his grand poem, Lucretius tells the story of Agamemnon's daughter, Iphigenia, who was ceremonially slaughtered by her own father in a sacrifice intended to placate the gods and make them stop the wind that was holding up the fleet full of heroes bound for Troy. Line 101 sums up Lucretius' feeling on this matter: *Tantum religio potuit suadere malorum* ("So strong was religion in persuading to evil deeds"). Even a modern translator quails at the line, translating *religio* as "superstition." Voltaire, who took the line straight, thought it would last as long as the world.[6]

Lucretius was wrong in many of his physical details, but that is only to be expected. What matters is that Lucretius had the scientific outlook, and science we know is self-correcting. Lucretius looked for answers in Nature, not in Religion. What Lucretius knew and what FitzGerald loved in him was the fact that Nature *is* the Law.

We can have some confidence in reporting FitzGerald's response to Lucretius because, in a letter to Cowell written in May and June 1848, FitzGerald called Cowell's attention to "the sad and grand lines from 569–580 of Book Two" of *De Rerum Natura*. Recent public events had been tumultuous. In 1846 the potato crop failed in Ireland; in 1847 there was a commercial panic in England; February 1848 saw barricades in the streets of Paris and Revolution again in France. FitzGerald read his Lucretius. "The ways of death can not prevail forever,/ Entombing healthiness, nor can birth and growth/Forever keep created things alive./There is always this elemental deadlock./This Warfare through all time."[7] "With the funeral dirge is mingled the wail that children raise when they first see the borders of light; and no night ever followed day, or dawn followed night, that has not heard mingled with their sickly wailings the lamentations that attend upon death and the black funeral."[8]

Lucretius is the only poet and the only philosopher FitzGerald discussed at length in the preface to the first edition of *The Rubaiyat of Omar Khayyam*. FitzGerald explicitly compared Lucretius and Omar, noting that "both indeed were men of subtle, strong, and cultivated intellect, fine imagination and Hearts passionate for Truth and Justice," and he noted that both "justly revolted from their country's false religion and false, or foolish Devotion to it." Of Lucretius FitzGerald observed that he "with such materials as Epicurus furnished, satisfied himself with the theory of a vast machine fortuitously constructed and acting by a law that implied no Legislator." Omar was then described by FitzGerald as "more desperate, or more careless of any so-called System as resulted in nothing but hopeless Necessity." Omar then "flung his own Genius and Learning with a bitter or humorous jest into the general Ruin."

The Lucretian note is everywhere in FitzGerald's lines, for example:

> *Oh threats of Hell and Hopes of Paradise!*
> *One thing at least is certain—This Life flies;*
> *   One thing is certain and the rest is lies;*
> *The Flower that once has blown for ever dies.*

John Ruskin said one's work should be the praise of what one loves. This is true for Lucretius, who loved the work of Epicurus; it is true for FitzGerald, who loved the work of Omar Khayyam; and it is true for those of us who have loved the work of Edward FitzGerald.

Chapter 26

FITZGERALD'S *RUBAIYAT* NOW

Now that FitzGerald's *Rubaiyat* has risen from neglect to sensation and sunk back to near neglect—not perhaps by ordinary readers, but certainly by the literary establishment—it is time to ask what the poem may have for us now in the twenty-first century. For our grandparents, late Victorians, the *Rubaiyat* was comforting and helpful. It recognized and validated feelings of loss, of longing, of nostalgia, of yearning. It had the melodic universality of the work of Amerian nineteenth-century songwriter Stephen Foster. It was emotionally open—but not too open—giving expression to desires that were still mostly hidden or ignored. FitzGerald's melancholy was not just an ache, it was a pleasure; his wit was a warrant and a preservative for joy; his yearning gave his readers reassurance that they could still feel, had not gone numb. The *Rubaiyat* urged its original readers to make the best of an empty heaven, to live all they could, to salute the dawn, seize the morning, take that glass of wine with lunch, and accept the coming of night.

My grandfather Richardson had FitzGerald's *Rubaiyat* by

heart so firmly he could recite it forward or backward. Born in
1870, he had come from Evansville, Indiana, had fallen in love
with languages, spent a year in Paris, then one in Berlin. He
learned Provençal, studied its poetry, and secured an instruc-
torship at Vanderbilt University in Tennessee. Then he met
my grandmother, who was unwilling to marry a poor professor.
To please her he quit Romance languages and made himself
over into an estate lawyer. Memorizing the *Rubaiyat* was his
way of hanging on to some piece of the life he had so romanti-
cally given up. He was a wonderful man, even-tempered,
constantly amused by life, warm, courteous, encouraging, and
fair-minded. I still think of FitzGerald's masterpiece as the
Rubaiyat of Emmet Richardson.

For Emmet's grandson's generation, the *Rubaiyat* breathes
a spirit that might in a pinch be spiritual but not religious
and certainly not fundamentalist. Omar's interest in wine is no
more consistent with strict Islamic practice than with strict
Methodism. FitzGerald's rejection of predestination and his
utter lack of interest in life after death set him at best on the
doorstep outside the church. FitzGerald's *Rubaiyat* came out the
same year as Darwin's *Origin of Species*, 1859, so one cannot say
the poem is Darwinian. But what is even more interesting
is that FitzGerald was responding strongly to one of the books
that most moved Darwin himself, Sir Charles Lyell's *Travels in
North America*. In this book Lyell gives a splendid and moving
account of how Niagara Falls proves the earth is vastly older
than the Bible chronology allows. As early as 1847 the thirty-
eight-year-old FitzGerald cited Lyell at length in an (unsuc-
cessful) effort to shake up his young Christian friend and future

Persian teacher Edward Cowell. "Lyell, in his book about America," FitzGerald wrote, "says that the falls of Niagara, if (as seems certain) they have worked their way back southwards for seven miles, must have taken over 35,000 years to do so, at the rate of something over a foot a year!" FitzGerald was clearly stirred by Lyell's essentially Lucretian argument, which he followed in detail. The age of the earth is to be read in the book of nature not in the Bible. "Sometimes they [the falls] fall back on a stratum that crumbles away from behind them more easily: then again they have to roll over rock that yields to them scarcely more perceptibly than the anvil to the serpent. And those very soft strata which the Cataract now erodes contain evidences of a race of animals, and of the action of seas washing over them, long before Niagara came to have a distinct current: and the rocks were compounded ages and ages before those strata! So that, as Lyell says, the geologist looking at Niagara forgets even the roar of its waters in the contemplation of the awful processes of time that it suggests."[1]

Lyell's understanding of natural processes gave the earth enough time for Darwin's natural selection to work: Lyell also gave FitzGerald a longer and older backdrop than that afforded to earlier poets. FitzGerald was well aware of it. His description of Lyell concludes, "It is not only that this vision of Time must wither the Poet's hope of immortality—but it is in itself more wonderful than all the conceptions of Dante and Milton." Let alone the Bible, he might have added, but didn't. FitzGerald had a great deal more sympathy with the new science than with the old religion, and Lyell—like Lucretius—is there in the *Rubaiyat*, in for example quatrain 47:

When You and I behind the veil are past,

Oh, but the long, long while the World shall last,

   Which of our Coming or Departure heeds

As the Sea's self should heed a pebble-cast.

The second great gift FitzGerald's *Rubaiyat* has for us now is its ungendered vision of love. The Persian originals available to FitzGerald mention houris—voluptuously beautiful women—from time to time; none appear in FitzGerald's quatrains. He knew, of course, that there are no gender-specific pronouns in Persian, no he or she, no his or hers, and he must also have been aware of the situation in the work of Sadi, Rumi, and Hafiz, in which, says the modern scholar Hamid Dabashi, "the uncertain gender of the beloved emerges as the destabilizing force . . . in which masculinity and femininity are decidedly undecided."[2] If FitzGerald was not able to recognize or directly express his feelings for other men, especially for young, good-looking men—and there is some disagreement about this—he was free to write about love as something more than gender-specific physical sexuality. So the *Rubaiyat* now reads like a large-tent gathering, an inclusive celebration of love with no group or groups stigmatized, marginalized, or excluded. This view of life can be seen simultaneously as FitzGerald's personal blind spot and as a liberating vision for modern love.

A third gift FitzGerald's *Rubaiyat* holds for us now is its sometimes calm, sometimes agitated, but always self-confident possession of the immense power of acceptance. FitzGerald accepts that one is in thrall, personally helpless, and in need of outside help, albeit with a bit of humor.

And much as Wine has played the Infidel
And robb'd me of my robe of honour—Well
I often wonder what the vintners buy
One half so precious as the stuff they sell.

There is a long Persian tradition of acceptance, as in Coleman Barks's fine version of these lines from Rumi:

Welcome difficulty.
Learn the alchemy
True Human Beings know:
The moment you accept what troubles
You've been given, the door opens.[3]

FitzGerald was able somehow to accept that things are not as well with us as they might be, and he was able to also accept the all-but-blasphemous notion that we can imagine, even if we have not been able to construct, a better world than this one. Third from the end, in all editions of FitzGerald's *Rubaiyat*, is this quatrain:

Ah Love! Could you and I with Fate conspire
To grasp this sorry Scheme of Things entire,
    Would we not shatter it to bits—and then
Remould it nearer to the Heart's Desire!

If we can accept that, it is only a short step to a belief in the power of imagination to place before us the world we most want. As the novelist James Salter has put it, "there comes a time when you realize that everything is a dream, and only those things preserved in writing have any possibility of being real" for those who come later.[4]

FitzGerald's *Rubaiyat* has two more gifts for the present age. One is the unfailing wit and good humor with which even the worst news is delivered. Referring to a hypothetical Creator, one quatrain incredulously implores,

> *Oh Thou, who didst with pitfall and with gin*
> *Beset the Road I was to wander in,*
>   *Thou wilt not with Predestined Evil round*
> *Enmesh, and then impute my Fall to Sin!*

FitzGerald lives up firmly and with a smile to Robert Louis Stevenson's saying "our business in this world is not to succeed, but to continue to fail in good spirits."[5]

And finally, to the extent that it is a faithful representation of its Persian originals—whether they were all written by the historical Omar Khayyam or not—FitzGerald's *Rubaiyat* shows us an approachable eleventh-century Iranian, a nominal Muslim, of probable Zoroastrian heritage, thinking about life and love in terms immediately comprehensible to an Internet-adept, scientifically inclined modern person. In the *Rubaiyat* of Omar Khayyam, one civilization speaks to another, as equals, across a thousand-year gap. In this instance, at least, words come first, then actions. Or, words are themselves actions. If we can begin with conviviality, we might end up with another Convivencia, the name given to the four-hundred-year-long stretch of history from the eleventh to the fifteenth centuries in which the Jews, the Muslims, and the Christians all largely got along with each other in Spain, or, as it was then called, Andalusia. Maybe we can live together. If so, it will not be in a political way or a religious way but in a personal way, and the personal way is what underlies and animates everything in the *Rubaiyat*. The *saki*—literally "cup-bearer"—of the last quatrain in the later editions (the same figure is called "sweet-heart" in the second edition) is usually taken to refer to the lover or companion who is left behind to offer the final salute to the true friend. The saki, the sweetheart who remains, can be of any gender, any nationality, can be anyone at all, can be you or me. We should drink to that, while we still can.

> *Yon rising Moon that looks for us again—*
> *How oft hereafter will she wax and wane;*
> *How oft hereafter rising look for us*
> *Through this same Garden—and for one in vain!*

> *And when like her, oh Saki, you shall pass*
> *Among the Guests Star-scatter'd on the Grass,*
> *And in your joyous errand reach the spot*
> *Where I made One—turn down an empty Glass!*

IMAGE CREDITS

page 9: Statue of Omar Khayyam in Nishapur, Iran, near his burial area. Permission is granted to copy, distribute, and/or modify this document under the terms of the GNU Free Documentation License, Version 1.2 only as published by the Free Software Foundation; with no Invariant Sections, no Front-Cover Texts, and no Back-Cover Texts. A copy of the license is included in the section entitled GNU Free Documentation License.

page 23: Sultan Alp Arslan. Bibliothèque nationale de France, manuscrit Français 232, folio 323.

page 29: Sultan Malik-Shah I. Public domain.

page 42: Site of the fortress of Alamut. http://creativecommons.org/licenses/by/3.0/

page 65: Mud walls of Nishapur, 1892. Public domain.

page 72: First edition of Edward FitzGerald's *The Rubáiyát of Omar Khayyám* courtesy of the Harry Ransom Center.

page 92: FitzGerald at Trinity, from drawing "Conic Sections" by Thackeray. Trinity College Library, Cambridge.

page 94: William M. Thackeray portrait by Samuel Lawrence courtesy of Bridgeman Images.

page 97: Painting of a young Alfred, Lord Tennyson by Samuel Lawrence courtesy of Getty Images.

page 106: Thomas Carlyle. Public domain.

page 113: William Kenworthy Browne, from an unfinished portrait by Samuel Lawrence.

NOTES

Chapter 1: OMAR KHAYYAM AND HIS *RUBAIYAT*

1   For the popularity of FitzGerald's *Rubaiyat of Omar Khayyam* see Garry Garrard, *A Book of Verse*, Stroud, UK: Sutton Publishing, 2007, esp. chapters 8 and 9. See also *FitzGerald's Rubaiyat of Omar Khayyam: Popularity and Neglect*, edited by Adrian Poole, et al., London: Anthem, 2011, esp. chapters 9 through 14. For Pound's letter see *Letters of Ezra Pound*, edited by D. D. Paige, New York: Harcourt Brace and Company, 1951, p. 180. For Pound's son's name see William Pritchard's December 17, 1988, review in the *New York Times* of *A Serious Character: The Life of Ezra Pound*, Boston: Houghton Mifflin, 1988. Pound said of his son's name, "Just note the crescendo." For Eliot's comment see T. S. Eliot, *The Use of Poetry and the Use of Criticism*, London: Faber and Faber, 1973, p. 33. A full and valuable treatment of Eliot and FitzGerald's *Rubaiyat* is Vinni Marie D'Ambrosio, *Eliot Possessed: T.S. Eliot and FitzGerald's Rubaiyat*, New York: NYU Press, 1989. The story about Bly came in an e-mail from Coleman Barks to the author June 7, 2014.

2 Edward Said's *Orientalism*, New York: Random House, 1979, holds that "the notion of an 'other' culture is of questionable use, as it seems to end inevitably in self-congratulation, or hostility and aggression." Simon Leys asks, reasonably, "why could it not equally end in admiration, wonderment, increased self-knowledge, relativisation and readjustment of one's own values, awareness of the limits of one's own civilization?" See Simon Leys, "Orientalism and Sinology," in *The Hall of Uselessness*, Collingwood, Australia: Black Inc. Press, 2012, p. 316. On the golden age of Islam and the contrast with the eleventh-century West see Maurice Lombard, *The Golden Age of Islam*, Amsterdam: North-Holland Publishing, 1975.

3 This is ruba'i number 5 in the Ouseley—or, as it is now called, the Bodleian—Manuscript 140 used by FitzGerald. The translation is the relatively recent one by Ahmad Saidi, *Rubaiyat of Omar Khayyam*, n.p., Asian Humanities Press, 1991, p. 66.

Chapter 2: THE LEGEND OF THE THREE STUDENTS

1 See Edward G. Browne, *A Literary History of Persia*, 4 vols. Cambridge: Cambridge University Press, 1928, vol. 2, p. 190.

Chapter 3: THE WORLD OF OMAR KHAYYAM

1 For details of the qanat water system, which exists again in modern Iran, see Terence O'Donnell, *Garden of the Brave in War*. Chicago: University of Chicago Press, 1980.

2   This is quatrain 41 in FitzGerald's fourth edition. Here and in subsequent references to Omar's quatrains, I give FitzGerald's version, but only if FitzGerald's version is a fair translation or representation of the Persian original. This book is for English readers. For those able to appreciate the Persian originals, the indispensable volume is *Edward FitzGerald's Rubaiyat of Omar Khayyam with Their Original Persian Sources*, by Edward Heron-Allen, London: Bernard Quaritch, 1899 (hereafter Heron-Allen, 1899). Heron-Allen reprints FitzGerald's fourth edition on each left-hand page, with the Persian originals in Farsi and in plain literal English on facing right-hand pages. This volume makes it easy for anyone to work from FitzGerald back to Omar. Edward Heron-Allen published another volume in 1898 called *The Rubaiyat of Omar Khayyam (A Facsimile of the MS in the Bodleian Library)*, London: H.S. Nichols, 1898 (hereafter Heron-Allen, 1898) which reprints the Ouseley (or Bodleian) Manuscript 140, a fifteenth-century Farsi manuscript accompanied by literal English translations and references to FitzGerald's versions of the Farsi originals. This volume makes it easy for someone to work from Omar forward to FitzGerald, while Heron-Allen, 1899 makes it easy to work from FitzGerald back toward Omar. English-speaking readers with little or no Farsi will find Heron-Allen, 1899 the more useful volume.

3   I give FitzGerald's rendering of quatrain 95 in the Calcutta Manuscript attributed to Omar. See Heron-Allen, 1899, pp. 30–33.

4   J.J. Saunders, *A History of Medieval Islam*. London: Routledge, 1965, ch. 9.

Chapter 4: THE EARLY YEARS
OF OMAR KHAYYAM

1   For the original Persian quatrains on which these lines of
    FitzGerald's are based, including the striking last line of
    each, see Heron-Allen, 1899, pp. 45–47.

2   Details of Omar's schooling are taken from Mehdi
    Aminrazavi, *The Wine of Wisdom*, Oxford: One World,
    2005. I have conjecturally given Omar's age when he was
    interviewed by Mawlana as twelve years old because another
    gifted contemporary, Abu Hamid al-Ghazali, entered his
    first madrasa at that age. See A. Bausani, "Religion under
    the Mongols," in *The Cambridge History of Iran*, vol. 5,
    Cambridge: Cambridge University Press, 1968, p. 289.

3   Max Rodenbeck, *Cairo: The City Victorious*. New York:
    Knopf, 1999, p. 57.

4   C. E. Bosworth, "The Political and Dynastic History of the
    Iranian World 1000–1217," in *The Cambridge History of Iran*,
    vol. 5, *The Saljuq and Mongol Periods*. Edited by J. A. Boyle.
    Cambridge: Cambridge University Press, 1968, p. 68.

Chapter 5: OMAR KHAYYAM AND THE COURT
OF SELJUQS

1   For an early modern interest in Omar Khayyam's work
    in mathematics, see M. F. Woepcke, *L'Algebra d'Omar
    Alkhayyami*, Paris: Duprat, 1851. For an excellent overview
    of Omar as a scientist, see A. P. Youschkevitch and B. A.
    Rosenfeld, "Al-Khayyami," in *The Dictionary of Scientific*

Biography. Edited by C.C. Gillespie. Scribner's: New York, 1973.

2 A.K.S. Lambton, "The Internal Structure of the Saljuq Empire," in *The Cambridge History of Iran,* vol. 5, p. 268.

3 Browne, *A Literary History of Persia,* vol. 2, p. 179.

4 "The Saljuq-nama of Zahir al-Din Nishpuri," in *The History of the Seljuq Turks,* translated and edited by Edmund Bosworth. London: Routledge, 2000, p. 63.

5 Carole Hillenbrand, "Aspects of the Seljuq Court," in *The Seljuqs: Politics, Society and Culture.* Edinburgh: Edinburgh University Press, 2011, ch. 2, p. 22.

6 Nizam al-Mulk, *The Book of Government or Rules for Kings,* translated by Hubert Darke. Richmond, UK: Curzon Press, 2002 (first published in 1960), p. 119.

7 The story about Mu'izzi is in Browne, *A Literary History of Persia,* vol. 2, pp. 35–37.

8 FitzGerald has made the lunch vegetarian. The Persian original gives "a loaf of wheaten bread," "a gourd of wine," and "a thigh-bone of mutton." See Heron-Allen, 1899, p. 23.

Chapter 6: OMAR KHAYYAM AND HIS
ASSOCIATES, 1075–1090

1 Marshall G. S. Hodgson, "The Ismaili State," in *The Cambridge History of Iran,* vol. 5, p. 427.

2 Marshall G. S. Hodgson, *The Secret Order of Assassins.* Philadelphia: University of Pennsylvania Press, 2005, p. 51.

3 Youschkevitch and Rosenfeld, "Al-Khayyami," pp. 323–34.

4   Omar Khayyam, "Being and Necessity," in Aminrazavi,
    The Wine of Wisdom, p. 285.

Chapter 7: THE DISASTROUS DECADE

1   See Heron-Allen, 1899, p. 25.
2   Marshall G. S. Hodgson, *The Venture of Islam*, vol 2.
    Chicago: University of Chicago Press, 1977, p. 185.
3   Ibid.
4   Heron-Allen, 1899, p. 45.
5   The anti-Hasan quatrains, if I may call them that, are numbers
    96, 43, and 45 in FitzGerald's fourth edition. See Heron-
    Allen, 1899, pp. 141, 69–71, and 73 to examine the Persian
    originals. The executioner—the ferrash—appears on p. 73.

Chapter 8: THE SUFI TURN

1   A. Bausani, "Religion in the Seljuq Period," in *The
    Cambridge History of Iran*, vol 5, p. 296.
2   Hodgson, *Venture of Islam*, vol. 2, p. 188.
3   See Heron-Allen, 1899, p. 101.
4   Paramahansa Yogananda, *Wine of the Mystic: The Rubaiyat of
    Omar Khayyam—A Spiritual Interpretation*, Los Angeles:
    Self-Realization Fellowship, 1990, reported by Aminrazavi
    in *The Wine of Wisdom*, p. 139. Dedicated seekers of alle-
    gorical and symbolic meaning may have no trouble with
    Yogananda's readings, but it is a problem that the stanza in
    question is one of FitzGerald's for which no close Persian
    parallel has been found.

5   Omar Khayyam, "On the Knowledge of the Universal Principles of Existence," in Aminrazavi, *The Wine of Wisdom*, p. 310.

Chapter 9: OMAR KHAYYAM'S RUBAIYAT

1   Aminrazavi, *The Wine of Wisdom*, p. 156.

2   A. Bausani, "Religion in the Seljuq Period," pp. 288–89.

3   The quatrain in question is number 31 in FitzGerald's fourth edition. He got it from quatrain number 314 in the Calcutta Manuscript sent him by his teacher Edward Cowell. The first line is "Up from Earth's centre through the seventh gate."

4   See Aminrazavi, pp. 92–93.

5   The notion of a Khayyamian School has been most persuasively put forward by Aminrazavi in *The Wine of Wisdom*, see esp. p. 98ff.

6   Browne, *A Literary History of Persia*, vol. 2, p. 18.

7   This and the rubaiyat that follow in this chapter are from the remarkable and valuable volume called *The Rubaiyat of Omar Khayyam* published in 1898 by Edward Heron-Allen, already referred to in chapter 3, note 2. The first part of the volume consists of Heron-Allen's English translation of all 158 Rubaiyat in Ouseley (now Bodleian) Manuscript 140. Next Heron-Allen gives a photographic facsimile of the entire Ouseley manuscript. Following that he gives a printed illustration of each page of the manuscript, accompanied by a transcription into Farsi, and further accompanied by the English rendition. So for any given quatrain in the Ouseley manuscript, one can see what the original

looks like, can make out the text in standard Farsi, and can see a literal English translation and a discussion of problematic words. Even a person with no Persian can grasp, from this volume, something of the process FitzGerald—or any modern translator for that matter—goes through.

8   Heron-Allen, 1898, p. vii.

9   Ouseley quatrain 5, in Heron-Allen, 1898.

10   Ouseley quatrain 151, in Heron-Allen, 1898.

11   This is Ouseley quatrain 155 in Heron-Allen, 1898.

12   This is Ouseley quatrain 158 in Heron-Allen's translation, in Heron-Allen, 1898.

Chapter 10: LATER LIFE AND LAST DAY OF OMAR KHAYYAM

1   A.K.S. Lambton, "The Internal Structure of the Saljuq Empire," p. 268.

2   See Aminrazavi, *The Wine of Wisdom*, pp. 30–31.

INTERLUDE: THE DESTRUCTION OF NISHAPUR

1   G. N. Curzon, *Persia and the Persian Question*. 2 vols. London: Longmans, Green & Co., 1892.

2   "Nishapur," *Encyclopedia Iranica*. http://www.iraniaonline .org/articles/nishapur-i.

3   Browne, *A History of Persian Literature*, vol. 2, p. 427.

4   Browne, vol. 2, p. 439.

5   Robert Byron, *The Road to Oxiana*. London: Macmillan and Co., 1937, p. 46.

6   Samuel Johnson, "A Criticism on the English Historians," in *The Rambler*, no. 122, May 18, 1751.

Chapter 11: LONDON, 1861: FITZGERALD'S *RUBAIYAT* APPEARS

1   Charles Eliot Norton, *North American Review* 109, October 1869.

2   Charles Eliot Norton, "Nicolas's Quatrains de Kheyam," *North American Review*, October 1869, pp. 575ff.

Chapter 12: FITZGERALD'S FAMILY AND EARLY YEARS

1   Robert Bernard Martin, *With Friends Possessed: A Life of Edward FitzGerald*. New York: Athenaeum, 1985, p. 75.

2   Alfred McKinley Terhune, *The Life of Edward FitzGerald*. New Haven: Yale University Press, 1947, p. 3. Details about FitzGerald's early years are mainly from Terhune and Martin, but I have also drawn from Thomas Wright, *The Life of Edward FitzGerald*, 2 vols., London: Grant Richards, 1904, and from Arthur C. Benson, *Edward FitzGerald*, New York and London: Macmillan, 1905.

3   The opening situation in this, the longest novel of any consequence in English, describes the newly wealthy Harlowe family, which uses money and marriage as tools to combine and augment land holding in a never-ending quest for a title and entry into the nobility; it is social climbing on a Himalayan scale. The protagonist, Clarissa, is as deeply

at odds with her family as FitzGerald was with his. *Clarissa*, as written by Samuel Richardson, is a million words long; first published in seven volumes, it is roughly the same length as the entire Harry Potter series or all of Proust's *In Search of Lost Time*. FitzGerald found time to read *Clarissa* five times—and indeed to produce an abridged version.

4   Terhune, p. 8.

Chapter 13: SCHOOL YEARS

1   Terhune, *The Life of Edward FitzGerald*, p. 13.
2   See FitzGerald's correspondence for 1833 in A. M. Terhune and A. B. Terhune, eds., *The Letters of Edward FitzGerald*, 4 vols., Princeton: Princeton University Press, 1980.
3   For a brief sketch of Spedding see A. M. Terhune and A. B. Terhune, eds., *The Letters of Edward FitzGerald*, vol. 1, pp. 59–61.
4   Terhune, *The Life of Edward FitzGerald*, pp. 16, 19.
5   The description is by Richard Monckton Milnes, in *Letters of Arthur Henry Hallam*, edited by Jack Kolb. Columbus: Ohio State University Press, 1981, p. 350.
6   "Frances Ann Kemble," www.univie.ac.at/Anglistik/easyrider/data/kemble.htm.
7   Fanny Kemble's best-known book is *Journal of a Residence on a Georgian Plantation 1838–39*. New York: Harper & Brothers, 1864.
8   Details of FitzGerald's physical appearance are from Martin, *With Friends Possessed*, esp. p. 79.
9   Terhune, *The Life of Edward FitzGerald*, p. 47.
10   Ibid., p. 32.

11 Ibid., p. 26.

12 Emma Leadbetter, "Tennyson at Cambridge," www
.english.cam.ac.uk/cambridgeauthors.

Chapter 14: THACKERAY

1 For the relation between Thackeray and Mrs. FitzGerald,
see Martin, *With Friends Possessed*, p. 58ff.

2 Ibid., p. 72.

3 A. M. Terhune and A. B. Terhune, eds., *Letters of Edward
FitzGerald*, vol. 1, p. 104.

4 Ibid., p. 153.

5 Martin, p. 181; Terhune, p. 257.

6 Quatrain 68 in the fifth edition.

Chapter 15: TENNYSON

1 A. M Terhune and A. B. Terhune, eds., *Letters of Edward
FitzGerald*, vol. 2, pp. 186–87.

2 Thomas Carlyle, quoted in Notable Names Database sketch
of Alfred, Lord Tennyson.

3 Terhune, p. 79.

4 *Letters*, vol. 4, p. 608.

5 *Letters*, vol. 1, p. 211, 290.

6 Ibid., vol. 1, p. 168.

7 *Letters*, vol. 2, p. 234.

8 This is the comment by David Perkins and W. J. Bate
in their introduction to Tennyson in *British and American
Poets, Chaucer to the Present*. New York: Harcourt Brace
Jovanovich, 1986, p. 518.

9   Quatrain 94.

10   The line in question is from quatrain 38 of FitzGerald's first edition. Details of this incident are nicely set out in Christopher Decker, ed., *Rubáiyát of Omar Khayyám: A Critical Edition*. Charlottesville and London: University of Virginia Press, 1997, pp. lii–liv and lx note 9.

11   Christopher Ricks, ed., *The Poems of Tennyson*. London: Longmans, 1969, p. 1318.

Chapter 16: CARLYLE

1   *Letters*, vol. 3, 651.

2   *Letters*, vol. 1, 211.

3   Ibid., 346.

4   Ibid., p. 351.

5   Ibid., p. 668.

6   Joseph Slater, ed., *The Correspondence of Emerson and Carlyle*. New York: Columbia University Press, 1964, p. 280.

7   Thomas Carlyle, *On Heroes, Hero-Worship, and the Heroic in History*. London: James Fraser, 1841, lec. 2, Mahomet.

8   Ibid.

9   Omar's original quatrains expressing difficulty in accepting predestination are fully as strong as FitzGerald's modern revisions. And since belief in predestination is a core belief of Islam, one has to wonder if Omar's expressions on this topic are what most offended the orthodox of his own era. See Heron-Allen, 1899, pp. 115–23.

10   *Letters*, vol. 1, p. 472.

Chapter 17: BACHELOR LIFE

1   *Letters*, vol. 1, p. 224.
2   Ibid., p. 517.
3   Terhune, *The Life of Edward FitzGerald*, pp. 87, 106.
4   Benson, *Edward FitzGerald*, p. 24; Terhune, p. 111.
5   Martin, *With Friends Possessed*, p. 61.
6   *Letters*, vol. 2, p. 264; *Letters*, vol. 3, p. 658–59.
7   Terhune, p. 337.

Chapter 18: A FRIENDSHIP LIKE A LOVE

1   Thomas Wright, *The Life of Edward FitzGerald*. 2 vols., London: Grant Richards, 1904, vol. 1, p. viii.
2   *Letters*, vol. 2, p. 296.
3   Benson, *Edward FitzGerald*, p. 14.
4   *Letters*, vol. 1, p. 153.
5   Ibid., pp. 121 and 215.
6   Ibid., vol. 1, pp. 225–26.
7   Ibid., vol. 2, p. 228.
8   Wright, *The Life of Edward FitzGerald*, vol. 1, p. 323.

Chapter 19: POETRY

1   *Letters*, vol. 1, p. 100.
2   Ibid., p. 122.
3   Ibid., p. 140.
4   Ibid., p. 641.
5   Ibid., p. 478.

6 Ibid., p. 246.

7 *Letters*, vol. 3, p. 410.

8 *Letters*, vol. 1, p. 308. This is a letter to Barton.

9 *Letters*, vol. 2, p. 3.

Chapter 20: FITZGERALD AT WORK

1 *Letters* 1, p. 633.

2 Terhune, *The Life of Edward FitzGerald*, p. 108.

3 Ibid., p. 230.

4 Ibid., p. 148.

Chapter 21: FITZGERALD AND PERSIA

1 George Cowell, *The Life and Letters of Edward Byles Cowell*. London: Macmillan, 1904.

2 The manuscript is described in Wright, *The Life of Edward FitzGerald*, vol. 1, p. 276.

3 Ibid., p. 291.

4 Terhune, p. 201.

5 Cowell's new find was labelled Calcutta MS 1548.

6 Terhune, p. 141.

Chapter 22: RENDERING *RUBAIYAT*

1 *Letters*, vol. 2, p. 224. It is noteworthy that Edward Cowell much later became one of Max Müller's translators, being co-translator of the next to last of the volumes of the *Sacred Books of the East* series.

2   *Letters*, vol. 2, p. 246.

3   *Letters*, vol. 2, p. 277.

4   This letter, complete with Farsi lines and words, is to be found in *Letters*, vol. 2, pp. 280–281. Literal translations by Edward Heron-Allen have been supplied by me in brackets. Translations or suggestions by FitzGerald are in italics. The two most useful books for identifying the Farsi originals behind FitzGerald's quatrains are, as I have said elsewhere in these notes, *The Rubaiyat of Omar Khayyam: A Facsimile of the MS in the Bodleian Library*, translated and edited by Edward Heron-Allen, London: H. S. Nichols, 1898; and *Edward FitzGerald's Rubaiyat of Omar Khayyam with Their Original Persian Sources*, collated from his own manuscripts and literally translated by Edward Heron-Allen, published in London by Bernard Quaritch in 1899.

5   See Heron-Allen, 1898, p. 123.

6   What FitzGerald was alluding to so delicately was Cowell's strong Christian side, his insistence, as he put it, on going to Nazareth not Nishapur for help. Cowell would maintain all his life that Omar was really a Sufi, meaning deeply religious. When Thomas Wright interviewed Cowell for his biography of FitzGerald, Wright asked Cowell about "Omar's laudation of drunkenness," which, said Wright, "is difficult to explain away." "By drunkenness," said Professor Cowell with a smile, "is meant divine Love." See Wright, *Life of Edward FitzGerald*, vol. 1, p. 278.

7   *Letters*, vol. 2, p. 323.

Chapter 23: TRANSLATED OR RENDERED?

1   The best recent account of the success of FitzGerald's
    Rubaiyat is Garry Garrard, *A Book of Verse: The Biography
    of the Rubaiyat of Omar Khayyam.* Two recent collections
    that give reliable accounts of the current state of *Rubaiyat*
    studies are Harold Bloom, ed., *Edward FitzGerald's The
    Rubaiyat of Omar Khayyam*, Philadelphia: Chelsea House,
    2004; and Adrian Poole, et al., eds., *FitzGerald's Rubaiyat of
    Omar Khayyam.*

2   *Letters*, vol. 2, p. 318.

3   Keeping track of differences between the early editions of
    FitzGerald's *Rubaiyat* has been a constant problem. Many
    modern editions give four or five of the early editions.
    Rubaiyat of Omar Khayyam, New York: Thomas Y. Crowell,
    1921, is an inexpensive and generally reliable volume. The
    best scholarly edition is Christopher Decker, ed., *Rubáiyát
    of Omar Khayyám: A Critical Edition.* This is a scrupulously
    presented text that allows easy comparison not only of the
    quatrains but of the introduction as it evolved under
    FitzGerald's hand.

4   *Letters*, vol. 2, p. 335.

5   See Friedrich Schleiermacher, "Über die verschiedenen
    Methoden des Übersetzens" [On the different kinds of
    translation], 1813, in *Sämtliche Werke*, vol. 2. Berlin: 1838,
    pp. 201–88.

6   William Aldis Wright, *Letters and Literary Remains of Edward
    FitzGerald*, vol. 3. London: Macmillan, 1889, p. 165.

7   Nathan Haskell Dole, *Rubaiyat of Omar Khayyam: English,*

French, and German Translations. Comparatively arranged in accordance with the text of Edward FitzGerald's version with further selections, notes, biographies, bibliography and other material collected by Nathan Haskell Dole. Variorum edition. Boston: Joseph Knight, 1896, p. xxxvii.

8   *Letters*, vol. 3, p. 339.

9   *Letters*, vol. 4, pp. 167–68.

10   Cowell's letter to Heron-Allen of July 8, 1898, is quoted in A. J. Arberry, *The Romance of the Rubaiyat*. New York: MacMillan, 1959, p. 20.

11   For quatrain-by-quatrain comparisons between FitzGerald's English and his Persian originals, see Heron-Allen, 1899. For a good treatment of Edward Heron-Allen and his work, see Garry Garrard, "Edward Heron-Allen: A Polymath's Approach to FitzGerald's Rubaiyat of Omar Khayyam" in Poole et al., eds., *FitzGerald's Rubaiyat of Omar Khayyam*. To assemble a collection of only those quatrains of FitzGerald's that are "faithful and beautiful" paraphrases of a single Persian Quatrain, take, from FitzGerald's fourth edition, quatrains 1, 6, 14, 15, 16, 17, 18, 19, 20, 21, 22, 25, 31, 36, 37, 40, 43, 44, 45, 52, 53, 55, 56, 58, 59, 61, 65, 66, 67, 68, 69, 70, 71, 75, 76, 77, 80, 84, 85, 90, 92, 94, 95, 96, 97, 99, 100.

12   See Dick Davis, "Edward FitzGerald, Omar Khayyam and the Tradition of Verse Translation into English" in Poole, et al., eds., *FitzGerald's Rubaiyat of Omar Khayyam*, p. 8.

13   See Aminrazavi, *The Wine of Wisdom*, pp. 11–12. He proposes we should speak rather of a Khayyamian school than of a historical Khayyam. Garrard reports that Ali Furughi accepted 171 of the thousands of quatrains attributed to

Omar Khayyam himself, while Ali Dashti considered 75 to be genuine and Sadeq Hedayat thought 120 were genuine. See Ali Dashti, *In Search of Khayyam*, translated by L. P. Elwell-Sutton, London: George Allen and Unwin, 1971; M. A. Furughi, *Rubaiyat of Omar Khayyam*, Tehran: Amir Kabir Publications, 1340 A.H.; and Sadeq Hedayat, *Songs of Khayyam*, Tehran: Amir Kabir Publications 1934 C.E./ 1313 A.H.

14   For Jewett, see Bloom, *Edward FitzGerald's The Rubaiyat*, p. 50, for Gosse, see D'Ambrosio, *Eliot Possessed*, p. 197; for Proust, see Anka Muhlstein, *Monsieur Proust's Library*, New York: Other Press, 2012.

15   Hamid Dabashi, "Found in Translation," *New York Times*, July 30, 2013.

16   *Letters*, vol. 2, p. 335.

Chapter 24: GERONTION: THE LAST YEARS OF EDWARD FITZGERALD

1   Benson, *Edward FitzGerald*, p. 171.

2   Ibid., p. 144.

3   Ibid., p. 142.

Chapter 25: THE LUCRETIAN PARALLEL

1   See Feldman's introduction to Rolfe Humphries's fine translation of Lucretius, *The Way Things Are*, Bloomington: Indiana University Press, 1969, p. 11.

2   *Letters*, vol. 2, p. 323.

3 Martin F. Smith, introduction to Lucretius, *De Rerum Natura*, translated by W.H.D. Rouse and M. F. Smith. Cambridge: Harvard University Press, 1976, pp. xliii–xliv.

4 Stephen Greenblatt, *The Swerve*. New York: W. W. Norton & Company, 2011, pp. 5–6.

5 Lucretius, *De Rerum Natura*, Book 5 ll 156ff.

6 Lucretius, p. 111.

7 The first five lines of this piece from Lucretius are from Rolfe Humphries's translation, *The Way Things Are*, pp. 67–68.

8 The second part of the "sad and grand" passage is from the translation by W.H.D. Rouse and M. F. Smith, *De Rerum Natura*, p. 141.

Chapter 26: FITZGERALD'S *RUBAIYAT* NOW

1 *Letters*, vol. 1, p. 566.

2 Hamid Dabashi, *The World of Persian Literary Humanism*. Cambridge: Harvard University Press, 2012.

3 *The Illuminated Rumi*, translated by Coleman Barks. New York: Broadway Books, 1957, p. 225.

4 James Salter quoted in Malcolm Jones, "A Changed Man," *New York Times Book Review*, April 28, 2013.

5 "Reflections and Remarks on Human Life" in *The Works of Robert Louis Stevenson*, vol. 16, Swanston Edition. London: Chatto & Windus, 1912, p. 363.

INDEX

Note: Page numbers in *italics* refer to illustrations.

INDEX

195

Wilson, H. H., 130
Wine of Wisdom, The
(Aminrazavi), 54
Wister, Owen, 85
Wister, Sarah, 85
Wordsworth, Christopher, 87
Wordsworth, William, 82, 83,
88–89, 100, 118, 120

Wordsworthian ideals, 5
Wright, W. A., 145

Yeats, William Butler, 58
Yerbudaki, Mahmud, 56
Yogananda, Paramahansa, 51

Zoroastrianism, 21, 68, 161

A NOTE ON THE AUTHOR

ROBERT D. RICHARDSON is the author of several books, including *William James: In the Maelstrom of American Modernism*, *Emerson: The Mind on Fire*, and *Henry Thoreau: A Life of the Mind*. He has edited several anthologies of poetry and prose, such as *Three Centuries of American Poetry* and *Ralph Waldo Emerson: Selected Essays, Lectures, and Poems*. He lives in Key West, Florida, and Cripple Creek, Virginia